CW00553696

WICCA

STARTER KIT

*Wicca for Beginners, Finding Your Path,
and Living a Magical Life*

LISA CHAMBERLAIN

Wicca Starter Kit

Published by **Chamberlain Publications (Wicca Shorts)**

ISBN-13: 978-1-912715-49-7

Disclaimer

YOUR FREE GIFT

Thank you for adding this book to your Wiccan library! To show my appreciation, I'm giving away an exclusive, free eBook to my readers—*Wicca: Little Book of Spells.*

The book is ideal for anyone looking to try their hand at practicing magic. The ten beginner-friendly spells can help you to create a positive atmosphere within your home, protect yourself from negativity, and attract love, health, and prosperity.

You can download it by visiting:

www.wiccaliving.com/bonus

I hope you enjoy it!

LEARN ABOUT WICCA ON THE GO

Want to learn about Wicca during your morning commute, or while doing your household chores? These days it can be difficult to find the time to sit down with a good book, which is why I'm thrilled to announce that all of my books are now available in audiobook format!

Best of all, you can **get the audiobook version of this book or any other book by Lisa Chamberlain for free** as part of a 30-day Audible trial. Members receive free audiobooks every month, as well as exclusive discounts. It's a great way to experiment and see if audiobook learning works for you.

If you're not satisfied, you can cancel anytime within the trial period. You won't be charged, and you can still keep your book!

To choose your free audiobook from over 20 books about Wicca and related topics, including best-sellers *Wicca for Beginners* and *Wicca Book of Spells*, simply visit:

www.wiccaliving.com/free-audiobook

Happy Listening!

INTRODUCTION

Congratulations on your decision to invest in the *Wicca Starter Kit*. Together, these three books provide a well-rounded entry point for your journey into the realms of the "Old Religion."

In this collection, you'll find in-depth discussions of the central beliefs, traditions and practices inherent to Wicca, practical tips for finding your particular path and integrating your new faith into your everyday life, and even a little spellwork for good measure!

The first book in the series, *Wicca for Beginners*, is the ideal starting point for anyone who is curious about the Craft. It's intended as a broad introduction, addressing the most commonly asked questions about Wicca.

You'll learn about the history of this fascinating religion, including its modern foundations as well as its ancient inspirations; the Wiccan God and Goddess and their multiple aspects; the Sabbats and the Esbats comprising the Wheel of the Year; core elements and tools of Wiccan ritual; basic principles of magic from both ancient and modern sources; and even an example ritual and spell suitable for beginners.

By the end of this guide, you will definitely have a solid understanding of the essence of Wicca!

Finding Your Path, the second book, is designed to help you with two crucial decisions faced by new Wiccans: whether to join a coven, and whether to follow a particular Wiccan tradition or chart a more individualized course for your practice.

You'll learn about the wide spectrum of contemporary Wiccan practice, from traditional "orthodox" covens to looser, more "eclectic" covens and circles, as well as the more recent phenomenon of solitary practice, which has appeal for both traditional and eclectic Wiccans alike. You'll also be introduced to the main Wiccan traditions: Gardnerian, Alexandrian, and Dianic, as well as a handful of other less common traditions.

If you don't already have a sense of the amazing diversity of this innovative religion, you certainly will after reading this book!

The final book in the series, *Living a Magical Life,* was created for new and aspiring Witches who want more insight and ideas for moving forward into full-fledged Witchdom. For many, this includes a formal initiation into Wicca.

Here, you'll find answers to commonly asked questions regarding coven initiation and solitary self-dedication, and a step-by-step solitary initiation ritual you can perform when (and if) you feel the time is right. But whether or not you make the choice to formalize your practice in this way, you'll find many valuable ideas and insights in this guide.

We'll also cover less-often discussed topics like navigating common obstacles along your spiritual path, leaving behind old beliefs that no longer serve you, and developing and strengthening your inner psychic guidance system. There are even a few spells and practices for staying stay in touch with your magical perspective every day—not just on Sabbats and Esbats!

Depending on your level of familiarity with Wicca, any of these books could serve as an excellent place to begin your dedicated study of the Craft. However, working through them in the order described above does allow you to build on your prior knowledge as you encounter new ideas and information.

That being said, as with anything related to the Old Religion, you should always listen to your own inner knowing—if you feel drawn to explore *Finding Your Path* first and return to *Wicca for Beginners* later, or if *Living a Magical Life* is calling you strongly, then go for it! No matter which order you choose, you will find yourself immersed in a wealth of knowledge about both the spiritual and practical elements of the Wiccan way.

May everything that you read within be of service to you on your journey, and Blessed Be!

OVERVIEW

The *Wicca Starter Kit* consists of the following three books:

WICCA

FOR BEGINNERS

A Guide to Wiccan Beliefs,
Rituals, Magic, and Witchcraft

LISA CHAMBERLAIN

CONTENTS

INTRODUCTION

If you're reading this book, you probably already know that Witches and Wiccans are *real* people, living in the contemporary world—not the mean, green-faced, scary old hags seen in popular movies and Halloween costumes.

They are not malicious, and they don't hex people or try to manipulate anyone through devious means.

Although many Wiccans and Witches may be secretive about their work and faith, there is nothing sinister about what they do. These stereotypes resulted from misconceptions about older, pagan religions found throughout Europe before the rise of Christianity, and while they may provide for good entertainment, they have also obscured the truth.

This has, unfortunately, prevented many people from knowing anything about the rich beauty of the traditions and the positive experiences for those following this spiritual way of life. Happily, you will soon know more about the realities, rather than the myths about Wicca.

In fact, interest in Wicca, Witchcraft, and contemporary magic has increased exponentially over the past few decades. This is at least in part thanks to the Internet. Just twenty years ago, people curious about these subjects might have had very little access to credible information, especially those without a good New Age or Occult bookstore anywhere in the vicinity. The internet has made information available to anyone who seeks it. Not every website is of equal quality, of course, and people are advised to disregard anything that doesn't "feel" right for them. This is true for print sources, as well.

No matter where you find your resources, you'll find that the more widely you read, the more varied the definitions, terminology, and even philosophy and beliefs involved in Wicca and Witchcraft become, as people writing on the subject come from a multitude of traditions and perspectives on the Craft. Wiccan authors can sometimes be an argumentative bunch—as people passionate about any religion can be—and you might find that some sources resonate with you more than others. Since there is no single authoritative source on the subject, it's up to you to choose whatever ideas and practices make the most sense to you.

This guide is intended as a brief introduction to the subject, covering the most basic questions that people curious about Wicca tend to have.

We'll be exploring the religion of Wicca, the history of its modern origins, and the basic beliefs systems that its various traditions hold in common. Then, we'll move on to magic, as we look at common Wiccan practices, including the relationship between Witchcraft and magic, and covering some of the common tools and rituals involved. Finally, I'll provide additional insights for those interested in learning more, borrowing from my own experience as a practicing Wiccan, and providing you with a sample ritual and spell suitable for a beginner, for those of you looking to practice magic.

Of course, no one guide can ever do a topic as diverse as Wicca justice, especially as every Wiccan has their own personal set of opinions and beliefs. For those of you wanting to learn more, I'll end this guide by suggesting several other points of reference for further reading, as well as sample tables of correspondence identifying the magical properties of selected colors, crystals, herbs and oils for you to experiment with, if you wish.

By the end of the book you will have a solid sense for the basics of Wicca and Witchcraft, and, I hope, a stronger desire to pursue this path.

Blessed Be.

PART ONE

INTRODUCTION TO WICCA

WHAT *IS* WICCA?

Before we get started, it's well worth establishing what Wicca really *is*.

Wicca is classified as a nature-based religion encompassing a wide variety of beliefs, traditions and practices inspired by many different sources—Wiccans often refer to these sources as "the Old Religion."

There are several different forms and traditions under the umbrella term of "Wicca," generally with overlapping elements such as pantheism, polytheism, an emphasis on ritual, and a deep respect for all living things.

Wicca has been described as a shamanic religion. "Shamanism" is a term originally used to refer to ancient religions found in regions of Asia, but it has since been used in reference to many indigenous traditions throughout the world, whose origins predate written history. Shamanism is often called the world's first religion, although it would not have looked like the major religions of today with their uniform beliefs and consistent practices that span continents.

Characteristics of shamanic traditions include an animistic world view, using altered states of consciousness to interact with the spirit world, and using the knowledge found there for healing and general well-being of the community. Shamans were the first "medicine people" and were revered in their societies. Like shamans, Wiccans seek connection with the unseen spirits of nature and work with natural agents such as stones and herbs for healing and protection.

Wicca is also considered to be a Pagan religion. Like "shamanism," "paganism" is also an umbrella term. It has been defined in the broadest sense as any religion that isn't Christianity, Judaism, or Islam, but it's more accurate to say that paganism involves nature-based belief systems that often (but not always) include several deities.

The word "pagan" comes from the Latin, where it meant "country person," and didn't have any religious association. Later, the word took on a negative connotation when Christianity tried to stamp out the old beliefs and practices of the country dwellers in Europe and other places it sought to dominate.

As a nature-based collection of beliefs and practices, Wicca is a type of paganism, but there are many other modern Pagan traditions besides Wicca. Some Wiccans resist the term and draw a clear distinction between themselves and Pagans. However, this distinction is aimed more at modern (or "Neopagan") spiritual movements than the general sense of the word as a category of "religion." What Neopagan traditions, Wiccan and non-Wiccan alike, have in common is an affinity with older, pre-Christian belief systems that may not be well-represented in written history but have retained a place in the human imagination, even if their particular expressions have morphed and changed over time. "The Old Religion" isn't found in a particular text or place or culture, but is a sort of catch-all name for the various strands of older cultural and spiritual beliefs that inform today's practices.

While it claims spiritual roots in older shamanic and pagan belief systems, Wicca itself is a *modern* religion, of relatively recent origins, and the use of the word "Wicca" as an official name for the religion came about several years after its initial founding. Since there is no consensus on any particular text, practice, or specific belief, there is a lot of leeway in terms of who might "claim" to be Wiccan, though many practices overlap among different traditions, groups, and individuals.

Among the many aspects of Wicca that distinguish it from other, more widely recognized religions is its emphasis on the feminine, as symbolized by nature, the Earth, the Moon, and feminine deities (or goddesses). The masculine is also represented through deity and is particularly associated with the Sun, but there is none of the patriarchy often found in other Western faiths.

Belief systems and practices identifying as Wiccan *can* be highly formalized and include hierarchical structures within practicing groups, but can also be very individualized and "free-form." The oldest forms of modern Wicca began with elaborately ritualized practice and hierarchical structures through which some Witches would rise through degrees of initiation to become High Priestesses and Priests.

Some covens today closely follow these original forms, while others have adapted and invented new forms, including more egalitarian structures. Some covens are for women only, while others are open to men and women. There are also an untold number of solitary Witches who prefer to practice alone. Some identify as eclectic, meaning that they don't follow any pre-existing tradition, but draw from many sources.

Wicca's modern history is full of interesting and unusual characters whose various contributions to the practice are a subject of much study and debate by today's historians of the movement. But before delving into the key points of Wicca's origins, let's look at some of the terms often associated with the name "Wicca."

Is Wicca *really* a religion?

In a word: Yes!

Although it is far less organized and visible than other faiths such as Judaism, Christianity, or Islam, Wicca has been recognized as being entitled to the same religious protections by courts in the United States, and is even included in the chaplain's handbook of the U.S. Army. In the UK, Wiccan priests and priestesses are authorized to function as prison chaplains, but Wicca is not officially recognized as a religion.

Wicca is sometimes referred to by those outside the practice as a "cult," possibly because it's called one in the Oxford English Dictionary. But this word is also tricky. "Cult" has several, neutral meanings, though unfortunately for Wiccans, it's often associated with negative images and groups with charismatic leaders like the followers of Jim Jones. Regardless, "cult" is not generally used by Wiccans to describe Wicca.

Most authors on the subject refer to Wicca as a religion, particularly those who identify as Wiccans. However, others who use the terms "Wicca" or "Wiccan" to describe their beliefs and practices don't necessarily regard Wicca as a religion that they follow or "belong to." This may be because Wicca has no central text, prophet, or other source of authority like the dominant Western religions, and its structures and forms of worship vary extremely widely. It may also be because the word "religion" has associations that some Wiccans are not comfortable with. (Many people in general will describe themselves as "spiritual" rather than "religious," and there's no shortage of Witches who do the same.)

For various reasons, the number of people identifying as Wiccans in predominately English-speaking countries is harder to accurately estimate than it is for more dominant religions. Many choose not to disclose their religion in a culture where it is not respected and is often enough even hostilely opposed. Others who might openly identify as Wiccans are uncounted, as there are no official houses of worship for them to be members of.

Nonetheless, some scholars reviewing random phone surveys over the past few decades have estimated that close to one million people around the world consider themselves Wiccans, with the majority found in the U.S. and the U.K. Whatever the actual count might be, it's clear that the numbers are rising steadily in the 21st century, as more knowledge about the religion becomes available and widely shared.

What's the difference between a Witch and a Wiccan?

Depending on who you ask, there's a big difference, or there's not much (if any) difference.

In terms of language, the words "witch" and "wicca" are related, as "wicca" was the Old English word that later became "witch."

However, among Wiccans the relationship between the two words is less black-and-white—there are Witches who identify as Wiccans, Witches who don't, and Witches who don't have a preference. There are also Wiccans who don't identify as Witches.

The varied uses of these words can be seen throughout contemporary writing about Wicca and Witchcraft. In addition to the name of the religion, some authors use "Wicca" as a singular word in place of "Witch," but most use "Wicca" as a plural term, meaning that several (or all) Wiccans can be collectively called "the Wicca."

Finally, while the words "Wicca" and "Wiccan" tend to be capitalized—especially in reference to the religion and its members—but there seem to be no hard and fast rules regarding whether to capitalize the words "Witch" and "Witchcraft" or leave them in lower case.

Some followers of Wiccan traditions who don't adopt the name "Wicca" as a personal identifier feel no need to identify with a capital "W" for "Witch" or "Witchcraft." Others feel that capitalization of these terms is important in distinguishing Wicca as an official religion and establishing a cultural respect for it as such. In the spirit of respect for those who feel strongly about recognizing Wicca as a religion, this guide capitalizes all four terms.

What's the difference between Wicca and Witchcraft?

Wiccans who don't identify as Witches don't use the term "Witchcraft" in association with their practice of Wicca—they don't use magic, and they draw a distinction between Wicca as a spiritual practice and individual relationship with the divine, and witchcraft as a practice that is not necessarily spiritual.

However, many Wiccans do blend magic into their practice to varying degrees, and may use "magic" as an interchangeable term with "Witchcraft" (often shortened to "the Craft") in association with Wicca.

In fact, some Witches who practice Witchcraft don't identify as Wiccan at all.

What does Wicca have to do with magic?

Once again, it depends on who you ask, and for Wiccans who don't practice magic of any kind, the answer is probably "nothing." However many, many Wiccans *do* include magic in their practice, to the point that the two are combined in many Wiccan books and resources—including this very guide!

Most Witches will refer to their practice of magic as Witchcraft, but may use either term. And of course, the word "magic" is also a bit tricky, as it has its own set of meanings.

"Ceremonial magic" is older than Wicca and was an original influence for what would eventually become Wicca, but it's actually a practice in its own right—in other words, not part of the religion. This ceremonial magic has several differences from the magic practiced by Witches. Ceremonial magic was derived from occult traditions through secret societies like the Freemasons and the Hermetic Order of the Golden Dawn, and is often quite elaborately ritualized. The term "high magic" is sometimes used to distinguish it from Witchcraft, which is called "folk magic" or even "low magic" by many of its practitioners. Some who practice ceremonial magic may identify as Pagans but are not Wiccans or Witches. Some simply identify as magicians.

What some call "practical magic" is a kind of ceremonial magic aimed at achieving common life improvements, such as healing physical or emotional ills, attracting love, and improving one's finances. Some Wiccans see this form of magic as non-spiritual and distinct from Wicca, but others blend the two by performing magic in alignment with their deities and for the good of all, rather than just for their own personal gain.

THE KNOWN HISTORY

The modern origins of Wicca can be traced back to the British Occult movement in the late 19th century.

A few key figures credited with developing and advancing Wicca as a religion are Gerald Gardner, Cecil Williamson, Patricia Crowther, and Lois Bourne. Gardner (1884-1964) is widely credited as being the founder of Wicca, although he and his fellow witches didn't use the term "Wicca" as an identifying term, but rather called their practice "Witchcraft," (sometimes shortened to just "the Craft") or "the Old Religion." Gardner did refer to the members of his tradition as "The Wica," but "Wicca" as a name for the religion was not used regularly until the 1960s as it spread to the U.S. and Australia.

Gardner had become interested in a theory advanced in the early 1920s by anthropologist Margaret Murray (1863-1963), which held that a pagan religion with a lineage going back to ancient times had existed in secret throughout the rise and domination of Christianity in Western Europe. Murray called this religion a "witch cult" and asserted that its practitioners were organized into 13-member groups, or covens, and worshipped a male "horned" god.

In the early 1940s, Gardner's exploration of mystical and occult experiences inspired him to develop a new incarnation of the witch cult, and he formed the Bricket Wood coven. Blending ideas from Murray with other sources such as Freemasonry, ceremonial magic, and the work of other Occult authors, Gardner's tradition expanded the deity worship to include a female goddess element along with the male god.

In 1947, Gardner met and befriended Aleister Crowley (1875-1947), a well-known occultist and writer who had explored and participated in a wide variety of religious and esoteric traditions from around the world, including Buddhism, Jewish mysticism, Hinduism, the Tarot, astrology, and more. Crowley's writings had a significant influence on Gardner, who included some of the rituals devised by Crowley in his own work. It was Crowley who coined the spelling of "magick" with a "k," to distinguish his form of magic from other "ceremonial magic"—and even stage magic—practices of the time.

Crowley is a complicated figure for many Wiccans today. Some of the practices he engaged in were considered to be scandalous, and his part in the history of the religion helped perpetuate an incorrect association between Wicca/Witchcraft and Satanism.

It should be noted here that "Satanism" is part of the Christian world view and not a pagan concept, and that Wicca does not, and never did, incorporate, endorse, or practice "Satanism" or the worship of anything "evil." Furthermore, Crowley had a reputation for being misogynist and racist, which are attitudes incompatible with the Wiccan way of life.

At any rate, the tradition now known as Gardnerian Wicca began to flourish as Gardner brought other interested Occultists into his coven, including several women, one of whom was Doreen Valiente (1922-1999). Valiente became the High Priestess of Bricket Wood in the early 1950s and revised much of the original material the coven had been using, in part because she felt it had too much of Crowley's influence. Eventually, Valiente parted ways with Gardner over what she felt to be his irresponsible attempts to make modern Witchcraft known to the masses, and his decision to limit the power of women in the coven in response to their criticisms.

Valiente formed her own coven in 1957, and went on to study Witchcraft with other leading figures in the movement, ultimately writing several influential books that helped launch the evolution of Witchcraft from a secret society phenomenon to a widespread, highly individualized practice. Other leading figures in the expansion of the Craft were Alex Sanders (1926-1988), who founded the Alexandrian tradition of Wicca, and Raymond Buckland, who formed the Seax-Wica tradition in the early 1970s. Born in 1934, Buckland is credited with bringing Gardnerian Wicca to the United States, and has written dozens of books on Witchcraft and other esoteric subjects.

It was during the second half of the 20th century that what is collectively called Wicca spread from England to the rest of the United Kingdom, and to the United States and Australia, branching out into several different traditions. While those who follow the Gardnerian traditions and its direct offshoots often draw a distinction between Wicca and other, non-Wiccan witchcraft, many people identify as Wiccans regardless of the origins of their particular practice. These include people following Dianic, Celtic, and Georgian traditions, as well as "eclectic" practices adapted from a range of traditions.

"Claiming" the Wiccan identity

One particular distinction often drawn between followers of Gardnerian and Gardnerian-inspired traditions and other kinds of Witches is the concept of "lineage." Gardner, who claimed to have received much of the knowledge he based his coven's work on from "ancient sources," performed rituals of initiation to formally admit new people to the secrets of the Craft, much like the Freemasons and other occult orders.

As Gardnerian Wicca grew and evolved, members of the Bricket Wood coven went on to form other covens and initiated new witches into the tradition. This practice was adopted by other off-shoots of Gardnerian Wicca, as well, so that today's Gardnerian (or Alexandrian, etc.) Witches can generally trace their initiatory "lineage" back to the early origins of Wicca.

As information and new ideas about Witchcraft spread, however, the requirements of initiation and lineage became less "absolute," and the options of self-initiation and solitary practice became popular for people who were interested in the Craft, but were unable (or unwilling) to join or start a coven. Solitary Witches may follow a specific tradition closely, or may create their own versions of Wicca from a number of sources, and may or may not even call themselves Wiccan. Many prefer the term "eclectic Witch" as a way of describing their "DIY" approach to Witchcraft, but even eclectics are likely to involve at least some elements of the more formal traditions of Wicca in their practice.

While it may seem to some that solitary or eclectic Witches can't be true "Wiccans" if they don't follow the set practices of Wicca as laid out by its initial founders, the flexibility and adaptability that draws so many to the religion was actually part of its inception. Gardner's original material was based on a combination of other, pre-existing sources, and was revised and added to throughout his own time. He was observed to have told his own followers that they should treat the Book of Shadows (his name for the collected material used in ritual and magical practice) not as a permanent text, but as something to add to and alter for themselves as they saw fit.

So there really is no true "doctrine" of Wicca to follow, and no way to truly "claim" the name at the exclusion of others, whether one is solitary or participating in a "lineage" tradition.

THE UNKNOWN HISTORY

Despite the claims of Margaret Murray, Gardner, and others to have discovered and revived an authentic ancient tradition, academic historians never could find much factual evidence to support the "witch-cult" theory. And within the movement, leaders' claims of trance states, being "descendants" of ancient Witch lineages or "reincarnations" of Witches from former centuries were sometimes doubted, even by other Witches.

It's possible that anxiety over the perceived degree of validity and authenticity of Wicca has caused some Witches to take strong stances in favor of one tradition over others, one belief over another, and to argue incessantly about it. It's also possible that these questions of authenticity led some Witches to draw more heavily from what is known about traditions from other cultures and other esoteric practices than from the specific material that was supposed to link the modern religion directly to its ancient past.

Yet, with all that is unknown about the past peoples and cultures that Wicca draws inspiration from, what *is* known is that there was *something*, some energetic phenomenon that was mystical and magical enough to keep a hold on humanity, even through the rise of Christianity and its eventual domination of the parts of the world most frequently associated with the "Old Religion." European folk magic traditions, many of which are incorporated into Wiccan magic, were possibly descended from this same source. And we also know that pagans and shamans of cultures around the world sought to interact with the unseen world in similar ways, through music, dance, and altered states of consciousness.

So it might be enough to say that what the original founders of modern Wicca did was create new forms through which people could tap into the mystical, bridging the gap between the ancient and modern worlds with new expressions of a magical energy that has always existed. There may be a dizzying variety of interpretations of these new forms, but there are enough commonalities among them, and enough people participating, to make it clear the "Old Religion" is back, and here to stay.

WHAT DO WICCANS BELIEVE?

Imagine an existence before "modern civilization" as we know it.

There is no electricity, no running water, no telephone communication, and no Internet (gasp!). You can't get tropical fruits in a supermarket in January even though you live thousands of miles from the nearest banana farm. There are no books, magazines, or newspapers. No weather forecasts, no news bulletins or alarms to warn of tornadoes, blizzards, or hurricanes. No calendars to mark the passing of the months, and no clocks to mark the passing of the days. And, perhaps most significantly, no environmental destruction anywhere near the scale we've been witnessing for the past few hundred years. Just the land, the water, and the sky.

Our oldest ancestors lived in this world.

They shared an intimate connection with the earth and the elements in a way we couldn't imagine today. They received information directly from the natural world and its turning seasons. Through the bounty of the Earth and the workings of the elements of rain, sun, air, and fire, they participated in the natural cycle of life.

They harvested the Earth's wild abundance to make food and medicine, and they worked with the Earth intentionally to create growth through crops and livestock. In the millennia before what we've come to call the Information Age, they learned what they needed to know about the world and its wonders from what their surroundings taught them. To survive their primitive circumstances, they had to pay attention.

And pay attention they did! Surviving ruins of ancient monuments around the world demonstrate the sophisticated knowledge our ancestors gained from studying the sky. The Mayans incorporated observations of the cycles of the Moon and Venus into their calendar systems. A pre-Celtic farming community in Ireland created an ancient temple mound with a passage that is illuminated only by the Winter Solstice Sun.

These accomplishments didn't arise solely out of close study, but were created in the context of a spiritual relationship with the cosmos. Mayan myths credit the god Itzamná with giving them the knowledge of the calendar system—and although we don't know the exact details, the ancient, unknown peoples of Ireland clearly involved a deity of some kind in their works.

The pre-written history of Wicca draws on the primal energy of this relationship to the natural world. Whatever the particular tradition or form the practice of Wicca follows, this connection with the forces all around us is the basis.

Wiccans know that although the world has been dramatically transformed by the impact of human presence, the basics remain the same, as our most essential requirements for survival have not changed. In this spirit, Wicca adopts and adapts its traditions both from what is known about our ancestors' ways of life, and from what is imagined, collectively and individually. The continuity may be considered symbolic rather than literal, but in grounding the Wiccan worldview in the realities of nature, Wiccans and Witches create a life of attunement with what some call "All That Is."

So Wiccans Worship Nature?

Wicca embraces the existence of two main deities, who are generically called the Goddess and the God, but who may go by a myriad of other names. They are, according to Wiccans, the original Deities, the female and male forces of nature that make all life possible. In one sense, Wicca can be called a duotheistic religion, though it's more complex than that, as many other deities from many ancient cultures are also likely to enter the picture (we'll cover this shortly!).

Some Wiccans believe that the Goddess and God are the *supreme* deities and all other gods and goddesses are lesser forms of deity. Others hold the perspective that the Goddess is comprised of all goddesses, and that each goddess is a particular aspect of the female power source, collectively called the Goddess. Likewise, all gods are individual aspects of the God.

Some traditions alternatively call these two deities "the Lord and the Lady," though in terms of its historical connotations, this pair of words implies a somewhat hierarchical, rather than equal, relationship— Wiccans believe the God and the Goddess are completely equal, although you may personally feel more affinity to one over the other.

For example, some eclectic Wiccans may, in their spiritual orientation to the divine, favor the male aspect of deity over the female to a degree, while others, especially followers of Dianic Wicca, pay far more attention to the female. Whatever the case, in its most basic form the relationship is between equals, as both female and male energies make up life on earth. In the natural world, one cannot exist without the other.

Representations of the Goddess and the God in Wicca tend to symbolize the principle functions of life creation that are the dominion of the female and male forces. The God is associated with the Sun, and also very often referred to and depicted as the Horned God. The Goddess, associated with the Moon, is actually comprised of three aspects—the Maiden, the Mother, and the Crone—which are represented by the cycles of the Moon. She is often called simply The Triple Goddess.

THE HORNED GOD / THE SUN GOD

Across many old European pagan cultures, a common deity appears, known as the Horned God, who is the ruler of wild animals and the hunting activities of humans. As a symbol of his connection with the animals of the forests and plains, he is often depicted with horns on his head, like those of the stag. He is also associated with the Sun and its role in the growing and harvesting of the food provided by the Earth. Older cultures called the God and Goddess the Sky Father and Earth Mother, identifying each deity's place in the continuation of the life cycle.

As the ruler of the Sun, the God is also associated with fire and light, and it is his journey around the Earth that shapes the cycle of Wiccan rituals in the year, beginning with Winter, then following the natural course of Spring, Summer, and Autumn, and back to Winter for the beginning of a new year. The Sun is said to be the source of all life, and so the God is also associated with sex, the procreative act that generates new life, and is often represented in phallic symbols such as the previously mentioned horns, as well as spears, swords, wands, and arrows.

Some of the deities from the world's pantheon who represent the God are the Greek gods Pan, Adonis, and Dionysus, the Egyptian Osiris, and the Celtic Cernnunos and Lugh.

THE GODDESS /
THE TRIPLE GODDESS

If the God, as the Sky Father, is the source of all life, the Goddess, as the Earth Mother, is the source that sustains life and allows it to flourish.

As a nurturing and tending essence, she is also associated with domesticated animals. Her realm of influence includes the Earth and its oceans, as well as the Moon that creates the tides. Other names for her include the Great Mother and the Divine Source. Symbols associated with the Goddess reflect the receptive aspect of sex such as the cup and cauldron, as well as her gift of abundance, such as certain flowers and fruits. In various Wiccan cosmologies, she may be represented by the Greek Diana, the Egyptian Isis, and the Celtic Brigid, among others.

As the female force that sustains life, the Goddess in modern Wicca is represented by three aspects which mirror both the life cycle of women and the phases of the Moon. Some written and pictorial representations from ancient societies show her as having three faces, one representing each aspect. In some traditions, she is called the

Triple Moon Goddess, recognizing the power source that is the Moon. In others, the balance of association with Earth as well as the Moon is reflected in the less specific name Triple Goddess. Each aspect of the Goddess has its role in the life cycle of the Earth and its inhabitants.

The Maiden

The Maiden aspect aligns with the crescent phase of the Moon. She is the growth phase of life, reflected in the waxing of the Moon as it moves toward fullness. She's associated with the season of Spring and with youth, innocence, and independence. Goddesses representing the Maiden include the Greek goddesses Persephone and Artemis, the Celtic Rhiannon, the Hindu Parvati, and the Nordic Freya.

The Mother

When the Moon waxes to full, the Goddess becomes the Mother, the source of the Earth's abundance. She's associated with Summer, and the lush time of year when plant and animal life matures into fullness. This is considered by many Witches to be the most powerful aspect of the Goddess. The Mother is represented by the Greek Demeter and Selene, the Roman Ceres, and the Celtic Badb and Danu, among others.

The Crone

The waning of the Moon belongs to the Crone, who is a symbol of death as part of the life cycle, and of the wisdom gained from a full and productive life. She is associated with the time of Autumn and Winter, the winding down and ending of the growing season. She completes the cycle of the Moon and the cycle of death and rebirth in all living things. The cycle begins again at the New Moon when the Maiden returns. Goddesses associated with death and the underworld often represent her, such as the Greek Hecate, the Russian Baba Yaga, and the Celtic Morrigan and Cailleach Bear.

EVERYONE ELSE

As was noted above, Wicca is more a polytheistic religion than a duotheistic one, since many different gods and goddesses may represent the Goddess and God. Furthermore, other deities can be part of Wiccan ritual in their own right, in addition to the main deities.

Many Wiccans cultivate individual, personal relationships with one or more deities from a range of ancient cultures across the globe, though most commonly from ancient Greco-Roman, Egyptian, and Celtic peoples. In this sense, Wicca is also a pantheistic religion, in that it is inclusive rather than exclusive when it comes to deities, and doesn't view the material world as inherently separate from deity.

The *encouragement* to find one's own personal relationships or affinities with deities of one's choice is another aspect of Wicca that sets it apart from most other religions.

People entering the Craft will study the myths and other known information and look for feelings of affinity with one or more deities in particular. They will also meditate on the possibilities and see which tend to "speak" to them on an intuitive level. Choices of alignments might be rooted in an ethnic or regional preference (for example, many Witches of Celtic descent tend to favor the Celtic pantheon), but are definitely not limited to these parameters, as the many aspects of deity are relevant to Witches for all kinds of reasons. Wiccans don't necessarily stay aligned with the same deities for their entire lives—new relationships may arise at different points in a person's life in response to new situations or circumstances.

In traditional Wicca, covens often center their worship and affiliations on one god and goddess as aspects of the deities. Members are free to have their own personal alignments with other deities of their choosing, but in formal ritual will work with the deities the coven is devoted to.

Understanding the Wiccan relationship with the deities begins with a look at how their holidays and rituals observe and celebrate the natural cycle of life. Ritual is where the most focused interaction with the Goddess and God takes place. Wiccans and other Witches pay homage to their chosen forms of deity and may work magical spells to bring manifestations of needs and wishes, both personal and collective.

THE WHEEL OF THE YEAR

Wicca is called an "earth" religion in part because its worship traditions are anchored to the natural cycles seen here on Earth, for example the turning of the seasons.

In an age when we are removed from nature by technological advances and endless distractions, marking the Wheel of the Year becomes a way to reconnect with the Divine essence of life and the Earth's role in our existence. Some Witches refer to their participation in the Wiccan holidays, known as Sabbats, as "Turning the Wheel," to emphasize our co-creative relationship with nature.

The Wiccan year is not the same as the standard Gregorian calendar, which begins on January 1st. Instead, it follows the four seasons, marking the progress in the Earth's path around the Sun (which appears, of course, to be the Sun's journey around the Earth) and the corresponding changes to life on Earth. Wicca has eight major holidays, or Sabbats, four of which are "solar holidays": the Winter and Summer Solstices, and the Spring and Autumn Equinoxes. The other four Sabbats, or the "Earth festivals," occur near the "cross-quarter days" between the solar holidays, and are based on older pagan folk festivals which are thought to have been linked to the life cycles of animals and agriculture.

Note: The dates for the solar Sabbats are given as a range to account for differences in the Sun's position in the sky relative to where one lives. The seasonal names for the Solstices and Equinoxes, as well as the seasonal associations with each Sabbat, are also different in the Southern Hemisphere.

The existence of eight Sabbats, rather than four, acknowledges that the contemporary delineations we mark between "the four seasons" are somewhat artificial. For example, Spring does not suddenly turn into Summer on June 21st—it has been moving in that direction for some time before the modern calendar recognizes it as "Summer."

In fact, an old name for the Summer Solstice is actually "Midsummer," recognizing that Summer has been well underway by the time the Sun reaches its zenith in the sky. The cross-quarter Sabbats mark the "seasons in-between seasons" and guide the ongoing transitions along the Wheel of the Year. The Sabbats are considered "days of power" and are marked by Wiccans, Witches, and other Pagans of many traditions.

THE SABBATS

Winter Solstice (Yule): December 20-23

Considered in most Wiccan traditions to be the beginning of the year, the Winter Solstice is a celebration of the rebirth of the God. It is the shortest day of the year, offering a welcome reminder that even though the cold season is still just getting underway, it doesn't last forever, as the days will begin to lengthen again after this point. Some consider the first Full Moon after the Solstice to be the most powerful of the year. This is a festive holiday celebrating light, as well as preparation for a time of quiet, inner focus as the Earth rests from her labor.

Among many Wiccans the holiday is more commonly called "Yule," a name derived from midwinter festivals celebrated by Germanic tribes. "Yule" is still referenced in modern Christmas carols, and many of the traditions surrounding the Christian holiday, such as wreaths, Christmas trees, and caroling have their roots in these older traditions. It was common for the Christian churches to "adopt" pagan holidays, repurposing them for celebrating saints or important events, as a way of drawing people away from the Old Religion.

Imbolc: February 2

Imbolc marks the first stirrings of Spring, as the long months of Winter are nearly past. The Goddess is beginning her recovery after the birth of the God, and the lengthening days signal the strengthening of the God's power. Seeds begin to germinate, daffodils appear, and hibernating animals start to emerge from their slumber. It is a time for ritual cleansing after a long period of inactivity. Covens may perform initiation rites at this time of new beginnings.

The name "Imbolc" is derived from an Old Irish word used to describe the pregnancy of ewes and has been sometimes translated as meaning "ewe's milk," in reference to the birthing of the first lambs of the season. It is also called "Candlemas," and sometimes "Brigid's Day" in Irish traditions. Associated with beginnings of growth, it's considered a festival of the Maiden.

Spring Equinox (Ostara): March 20-23

At the Spring Equinox, light and dark are finally equal again, and growth accelerates as both the light from the still-young God of the Sun and the fertility of the Earth grow more powerful. Gardening begins in earnest and trees send out blossoms to participate with the pollinating bees. The equal length of day and night brings about a time for balancing and bringing opposing forces into harmony.

The name "Ostara" comes from the Saxon Eostre, the Goddess of Spring and renewal. This is where the name Easter comes from, as this is another holiday that was "merged" with the Christian tradition.

Beltane: May 1

As Spring begins to move into Summer, the Goddess begins making her transition into the Mother aspect, and the God matures into his full potency. Beltane is a fire festival, and a celebration of love, sex, and reproduction. It's at this time that the Goddess couples with the God to ensure his rebirth after his death at the end of the life cycle. Fertility is at its height and the Earth prepares to flourish with new life.

The name "Beltane" comes from an ancient festival celebrated throughout the Celtic Isles that marked the beginning of Summer, and is derived from an old Celtic word meaning "bright fire." The ancient Irish would light giant fires to purify and protect their cattle, and jumping over fires was considered a way to increase fertility and luck in the coming season.

Summer Solstice / Midsummer: June 20-23

Long considered one of the most magical times of the year, the Summer Solstice sees the God and the Goddess at the peak of their powers. The Sun is at its highest point and the days are at their longest. This is a celebration of the abundance of sunlight and warmth, and the physical manifestation of abundance as the year heads toward the first of the harvests. It's a time of ease and of brief rest after the work of planting and before the work of harvesting begins.

Some traditions call this Sabbat "Litha," a name traced back to an old Anglo-Saxon word for this time of year.

Lammas: August 1

Lammas marks the beginning of the harvest season. The first crops are brought in from the fields, the trees and plants begin dropping their fruits and seeds, and the days are growing shorter as the God's power begins to wane. This is a time for giving thanks for the abundance of the growing season as it begins to wind down.

The word Lammas stems from an old Anglo-Saxon word pairing meaning "loaf mass," and it was customary to bless fresh loaves of bread as a way of celebrating the harvest. Lammas is alternately known as "Lughnasa," after the traditional festivals in Ireland and Scotland held at this time to honor the Celtic god Lugh, who was associated with the Sun.

Autumn Equinox (Mabon): September 20-23

The harvest season is still in focus at the Autumn Equinox. The animals born during the year have matured, and the trees are beginning to lose their leaves. Preparations are made for the coming winter. The God is making his exit from the physical plane and heading toward his mythical death at Samhain, and his ultimate rebirth at Yule. Once again, the days and nights are of equal length, symbolizing the temporary nature of all life—no season lasts forever, and neither dark nor light ever overpowers the other for long. As with the Spring Equinox on the opposite side of the Wheel, balance is a theme at this time.

The Autumn Equinox is considered in some traditions to be "the Second Harvest," with Lammas as the first and Samhain as the last of three harvests. A more recent name for the holiday is "Mabon," after a Welsh mythological figure whose origins are connected to a divine "mother and son" pair, echoing the dual nature of the relationship between the Goddess and the God.

Samhain: October 31

Considered by many Wiccans to be the most important of the Sabbats, Samhain is the time when the part death plays in the cycle of life is acknowledged and honored. The word "Samhain" comes from old Irish and is thought by many to mean "Summer's end," though others trace it to a root word meaning "assembly," which may refer to the communal gathering of a pagan festival, especially during the harvest season. As the Sun aspect, the God retreats into the shadows as night begins to dominate the day. As the God of the Hunt, he is a reminder of the sacrifice of life that keeps us alive through the long winter months. The harvest is complete and the sacred nature of food is respected. Among some traditions this is viewed as the "Third Harvest."

Wiccan and other pagan traditions view Samhain as a point in the Wheel when the "veil" between the spiritual and material worlds is at its thinnest, and the days around Samhain are considered especially effective for divination activities of all kinds. Ancestors are honored and communicated with at this time. Many of the Halloween traditions still celebrated in contemporary cultures today can be traced back through the centuries to this festival. Pagans of the old times left food offerings for their ancestors, which became the modern custom of trick-or-treating. Jack-o-lanterns evolved from the practice of leaving candle-lit hollowed-out root vegetables to guide spirits visiting on Earth.

Some Wiccans in the Celtic traditions consider Samhain, as opposed to Yule, to be the beginning of the year, as the death and rebirth aspects of creation are seen to be inherently joined together—death opens the space for new life to take root. Honoring the ancient Celtic view of the year having a "light half" and a "dark half," their Wheel of the Year begins anew on this day, the first day of the dark half of the year.

THE ESBATS

In addition to the Sabbats, the Wiccan year contains 12 (sometimes 13) Full Moon celebrations, known as the Esbats. While the Sabbats tend to focus celebration on the God and his association with the Sun, the Esbats honor the Goddess in her association with the Moon. Covens traditionally meet on the Esbats to celebrate a particular aspect of the Goddess, such as Aphrodite, in a celebration of abundance, or Persephone, in a ritual for renewal. They work with the Goddess to bring about healing and assistance for their members and communities, and often work for the good of the wider world as well.

The Full Moon is also seen within the context of the Wheel of the Year, with names and seasonal attributions for each. For Wiccans working with particular aspects of the Goddess, the specific goddess called upon during an Esbat will often correspond with the time of year. For example, Aphrodite is an appropriate goddess to celebrate abundance under a Summer Moon, whereas Persephone, with her underworld associations, is more appropriate to work with under a late Autumn or early Winter Moon.

The names for each Moon may vary from tradition to tradition, but are generally related to the time of year and the corresponding level of abundance and activity of life on Earth, as well as the Sun's point in its journey around the Earth. In the Northern Hemisphere, the most typical names for the Full Moons in Wiccan rituals are as follows:

Month	Moon Name
January	Cold Moon (also Hunger)
February	Quickening Moon (also Snow)
March	Storm Moon (also Sap)
April	Wind Moon (also Pink)
May	Flower Moon (also Milk)
June	Sun Moon (also Strong Sun and Rose)

Month	Moon Name
July	Blessing Moon (also Thunder)
August	Corn Moon (also Grain)
September	Harvest Moon
October	Blood Moon
November	Mourning Moon (also Frost)
December	Long Nights Moon

Many Witches consider astrological influences in addition to seasonal influences and will work according to the particular sign the Moon is in while full. They will refer to the Moon accordingly, such as the "Gemini Moon" or the "Aquarius Moon."

When more than one Full Moon occurs in a given calendar month, it's called a Blue Moon. Occurring roughly once every two and a half years, this is considered a particularly powerful time in many Wiccan traditions, and special attention is paid to working with the rare energy of a Blue Moon.

THE ELEMENTS

One way of connecting with the energies of the natural world, and by extension, the entire Universe, is in relationship with the Four Elements.

The recognition of elemental states of matter has been around since the ancient Greeks, and versions of the concept appear in a number of cultures with ancient lineages. In Wicca and other pagan belief systems, the Elements are seen as fundamental aspects of divine energy, each containing qualities that manifest in our personalities and our way of being in the world. They are an important component of Wiccan ritual, where each element is represented in the tangible forms of colors, tools, natural objects, instruments and herbs, and the intangible forms of the four cardinal directions, the four seasons, particular deities, and, often, astrological signs.

Working with the Elements can help increase certain desired energies and experiences such as love and abundance, and can help balance unwanted experiences rooted in the negative qualities inherent in personalities.

Let's take a look at the four elements, in turn.

Earth

The Earth is the center of our human universe, providing us the foundation of life and keeping us literally grounded through its gravitational pull. It's the source of all sustaining plant and animal life that provide nourishment and healing. It can cause physical death and destruction through earthquakes, mudslides and avalanches.

The Earth is physically represented by many of its topographical features, such as rocks, soil, caves, fields, forests, and gardens. The Element of Earth is associated with strength, abundance, and prosperity, and is represented by the colors green, yellow, brown, and black. Earth energy is feminine and receptive. Positive qualities associated with Earth are stability, responsibility, respect, and endurance, while negative qualities include stubbornness and rigidity. The Earth's cardinal direction is North, and its season is Winter.

Air

Air is the invisible Element. Its presence is only seen in the effects it has on other matter—leaves fluttering in the breeze, the movement of the clouds. Although it can't be seen itself, it can be felt all around us, which may be why it's associated with the mind, the intellect, communication and divination.

It's also associated with sky, wind, mountaintops and birds, and is represented in yellow, white, and silver, among other colors. Air is essential for life as it carries oxygen, and it contributes to abundance by carrying and spreading seeds to new places where they can sprout. It also participates in the destructive force of life with storms and frigid wind. It is a masculine, projective energy. Positive personal qualities associated with Air energy include intelligence, inspiration, and optimism. Negative qualities include gossip and forgetfulness. Air's cardinal direction is East, and its season is Spring.

Fire

The awesome, destructive potential of Fire is probably most striking in the seasonal wildfires that burn millions of acres of forest around the world, and can actually jump over rivers and roads to resume their spread on the other side. Lightning can also be deadly, as can extreme heat. Of course, Fire is also life-sustaining, used for cooking and lighting for over 100,000 years.

The Element of Fire is associated with the Sun, sunlight, stars, deserts, and volcanoes. It is represented with red, gold, crimson, orange, and white, and is a masculine, projective energy. Fire is the Element of transformation illumination, health, and strength. Its positive qualities promote love, passion, enthusiasm, courage, and leadership. Negative qualities include hate, jealousy, fear, anger, and conflict. Its season is Summer, and South is its cardinal direction.

Water

Water is essential for life on Earth and is present in all life. It established forms in the Earth such as lakes and rivers by following the path of least resistance, and can wear away solid rock over time. It is associated with all of its visible physical manifestations, such as streams, springs, oceans, the rain, and the Moon, which exerts its own gravitational pull on Water's most massive forms. Its destructive forces manifest in severe rainstorms, floods, whirlpools and riptides.

Its Elemental energy is associated with emotions, healing, dreams, psychic clairvoyance and the subconscious. Water is receptive, feminine, and represented by blue, green, indigo and black. Its positive qualities include compassion, forgiveness, and intuition. Negative qualities are laziness, indifference, insecurity, and lack of control over emotions. Autumn is Water's season, and its cardinal direction is West.

The Fifth Element: Spirit

Many Wiccan traditions recognize a Fifth Element which is referred to as "Aether," or, more commonly, "Spirit."

This is the Element present in all things, immaterial but essential for connection and balance between all other Elements. It has been described as the binding force through which manifestation is made possible, as well as the divine intelligence of the "All" that spiritualists of many traditions seek connection with. The Fifth Element is also known as "Akasha," from the Sanskrit word for "aether," which is found in Buddhism, Hinduism, and other religions, and is translated by some as "inner space" or "open space."

The Fifth Element is represented by the color white. Unlike the other Elements, it has no gender, energy type, or cardinal direction. It has no season, but is rather associated with the entire Wheel of the Year.

OTHER BELIEFS

Borrowing as it does from many older spiritual traditions, Wicca is inherently a "patch-worked" system of beliefs. In addition to relationship with deity and the participation in the natural cycles of life, other beliefs and practices contribute to the Wiccan religion.

These beliefs are as personal and idiosyncratic as the choice of deities one resonates with, and include reincarnation, animism, the existence of unseen dimensions, sometimes called "the Otherworld," and the existence of fairies and/or other unseen spirits.

REINCARNATION

A major tenet among Wiccans, the idea that we live many times over in different times and places on Earth is found in several religions, including Jainism, Hinduism, and Buddhism, as well as in other ancient and modern cultures.

Wicca has adopted this belief in many ways, which differ from coven to coven and individual to individual. While some Witches believe that we can and sometimes do choose to reincarnate in non-human forms—i.e. as animals or plants—many others believe that we only come back as humans.

Either way, reincarnation is seen as a logical extension of the life/death/life cycle observed in nature and celebrated throughout the Wheel of the Year. It is also used as a lens through which to look at life struggles and lessons, as the belief that we've chosen our life circumstances before being born into our new bodies is common.

While it's never possible to scientifically verify the existence of past lives, many Wiccans and other spiritual seekers feel to be aware of at least some details of a past before this life, while others may have a sense of having "been here" before. This feeling may occur in or near a particular place where a past life was lived, or manifest in an affinity for a particular time period in history or a country or continent that has never been visited in this lifetime. A common "past life history" among Witches involves at least one prior life as a Witch, often one that ended in some form of persecution. Many of these Witches feel they have chosen to come back at a time when their form of religion is accepted—at least enough not to put them in real danger.

Wiccans and spiritual healers of many traditions today employ meditation, past-life regression, and dream analysis techniques to help people recall their past lives as a way of understanding their current problems. It is thought that whatever spiritual lessons were not learned in the past can be actively worked on in this life, which sets up the soul to learn new lessons, both in this and future lives.

THE AFTERLIFE

Wiccans generally believe in an afterlife of some form or another. However, this is not an "absolute" place where we remain for eternity—for example the Christian Heaven and Hell—but rather the place where our souls spend time between incarnations.

Names and descriptions for this realm vary widely and may be based on older belief traditions or be more idiosyncratic, with each individual's experience and perception informing her or his notion of what's beyond that which we can physically perceive as this life. The spiritual realm is known as the Otherworld, the Afterworld, Summerland, and the Shining Land, among other names. Some describe it as a naturally abundant and beautiful place, while others see it more as an entity that doesn't resemble any physical reality on Earth.

It is nevertheless interconnected with all things in the Universe and many who practice divination believe it to be the source of the answers to their questions. It is thought by some Wiccans that the afterlife is a place to make choices about our next incarnations based on what we've learned, or haven't yet learned, so far in our soul's journey.

ANIMISM

In its most basic form, animism is the belief that everything in the material world has a "soul" or a "spirit." This applies to all non-human animals as well as the geographical and ecological phenomena of rocks, trees, and anything else found on Earth. Many indigenous cultures operate from an animistic perspective, including several Native American belief systems and the traditional Japanese Shinto religion.

Animism provides a way of seeing into the divine relationship between humans and the natural world, as particular stones, trees, and streams may be imbued with a special sense of energy and held as sacred sites of worship. The Celtic belief in fairies (also spelled "faeries") can be seen as a form of animism, as they are themselves generally invisible but thought to live in hills, mounds, woodlands, and other natural phenomena.

For some, animism also powers the workings of magic, as objects used in ritual may be thought to possess their own spirit energies, which are joined with those of the Witch to effect the positive change being sought.

OTHER OCCULT SYSTEMS

The ancient traditions of astrology provide a way to view events on Earth as being influenced by the energies and locations of celestial bodies. Astrological systems vary from culture to culture, but Wicca tends to incorporate Western astrology with its focus on the Sun, the Moon, the planets of our Solar System, and the other stars of the Milky Way Galaxy.

The signs of the Zodiac wheel, which measures the Sun's path across the celestial sphere according to how it looks from Earth, are named for constellations and assigned "ruling" planets that influence behavior and phenomena in particular ways. The horoscopes that most people are familiar with today represent only a fraction of the information contained in astrology, as they tend to focus solely on a person's Sun sign. The full picture of a person's personality makeup and potential life paths is much more complex.

Many Wiccans know at least the basics of their astrological birth charts—their Sun sign, Moon sign and Rising sign—as well as the general "personality type" of each sign in the Zodiac wheel. The current position of both the Sun and Moon at any given time is often taken into consideration when working magic for a particular purpose. The Moon's current sign is especially important for Esbats, with different signs being more or less favorable for specific intentions. And some Witches mark the four Earth Sabbats (Imbolc, Beltane, Lammas, and Samhain) by the zodiacal midpoint between the nearest solar holidays, or "cross quarter" days, rather than on the modern calendar dates, so that Beltane, for example, is celebrated on February 4th instead of February 2nd.

Numerology is an occult system of assigning spiritual and/or magical qualities to the numbers 0-9 (and, in some traditions, 11 and 22). Each number has its own energy and characteristics that manifest as personality traits and life experiences.

For example, people who are assigned the number 6 based on the date of their birth or the letters in their names are said to be very family oriented, and their lives will reflect this. Numerological significances can be incorporated into Wiccan practice in ritual, magic, and divination methods. The number 3 is particularly significant to Wiccans, as seen in the many versions of the Triple Goddess. Some Wiccans choose a sacred "Wiccan name" for themselves based on numerological systems.

Finally, different methods and traditions of divination are often part of Wiccan practice. Witches use Tarot cards, pendulums, runes, the Celtic Ogham, and objects for "scrying" such as crystal balls, mirrors, and the surface of still water to communicate with unseen energies and discover the hidden forces at work in their unfolding lives.

Witches might consult their preferred divination tools for insight into how best to set their intentions for a coming ritual. Divination may also be part of ritual or occur immediately after, but can be practiced at any time. Astrology and numerology are often intertwined with certain divination practices, especially in Tarot and other forms of divination cards.

THE NEXT STEP

Now that we've taken a brief look at the origins and the basic belief systems of modern Wicca, let's take a closer look at how these belief systems are enacted through religious ritual, magical spellwork, and general daily life.

PART TWO
INTRODUCTION TO WITCHCRAFT

WHAT IS WITCHCRAFT?

As noted previously, those who identify as Wiccans and those who identify as Witches have differences of opinion regarding the term "Witchcraft." While not all Witchcraft is considered to be specifically "Wiccan," the terms "Wicca" and "Witchcraft" are often used interchangeably.

Some Wiccans argue for a distinction between what they consider to be spirituality-based worship ("Wicca") and more "secular" magical practice ("Witchcraft"), but more often the two are intertwined enough that the distinction isn't particularly useful.

With all due respect to Wiccans who recognize a difference, the term "Witchcraft" will be used in this guide to describe the general activities found in rituals practiced by Wiccans and non-Wiccan Witches alike. Because some Wiccans do not practice magic and do not consider themselves Witches, the term "Witch" in this section of the guide is meant to refer those who both adopt Wiccan practices in some form or another *and* practice magic as part of their religion.

Still with me? Great, let's take a look at Witchcraft and magic in more detail.

Witchcraft is the set of beliefs and practices employed by Witches in ritual and spellwork. Often, magical work is incorporated into the Sabbat and Esbat celebrations observed by covens and solitary Witches, though spellwork may be employed on its own on other occasions. In fact, many Witches consider themselves to be constantly "practicing" their Craft in their daily lives through the use of

49

meditation, magically charged meals and beverages, color choices in clothing and jewelry, nightly candle rituals, and other seemingly "small" enactments of magic. The more one is in tune with the rhythms and energies of the natural world, the more "magical" one's life will seem and feel, and this relationship with the cycles of life is deepened throughout one's life through study and practice.

"Magic" is a word used for the phenomena that occur when people consciously participate in the co-creative forces of the Universe, by using the subtle energies of nature to cause desired change in their reality.

People may use magic, or "the Craft" as it is often called, for many purposes. This often includes spells, charms, and other workings for what could be called "personal gain," such as a new job or improvements in a love relationship. However, the Craft is also used to work for benefits to one's family, community, or even to people across the globe. For example, a coven may use an Esbat ritual as an opportunity to send beneficial healing light to victims of a natural disaster. What the Craft is definitely *not* used for is anything that would cause harm to another person or other living being, even unintentionally. Our wishes can often be manipulative when it comes to how they affect other people, even when we don't realize it. Therefore, ritual and spellwork often include safeguards against accidental misuse of magical energy, such as the phrases "for the good of all" and "harm to none"—taken from the Wiccan rede. Keeping this idea in the forefront of one's mind is important, particularly in light of another basic tenet of Witchcraft: the Threefold Law.

Also known as "The Rule of Three" and "The Law of Return," this principle states that whatever Witches send out into the Universe as intent, whether positive or negative, will come back to them three times as great. While some Witches don't subscribe to this particular belief, it is often invoked as a reminder that magical power should be used only for good, and never in the spirit of harm or manipulation.

MAGIC AND SCIENCE

Many contemporary writers on Witchcraft have pointed out the relevance of new discoveries in the physical sciences that seem to identify what Witches have always known to exist: a symbiotic relationship between mind and matter.

This relationship can be viewed from many angles and is probably not entirely understood by anyone, but its existence is clear to practitioners of magic as well as other mind/thought-based disciplines that bring about positive change in one's life.

The traditional worldview of most of Western society for the past few millennia has held that reality is chaotic and inflexible, created by forces outside of human control. It has also held that the mind is not a physical entity, and is separate from what we think of as "matter." (The phrase "mind over matter" illustrates the fundamental opposition perceived to exist between the two.) What Witches understand, and what science has begun to uncover, is that reality is flexible, and *is* co-created by and with everything in it, including the mind. Mind is not separate from matter, but *is* matter in its most basic form.

The power of thought has been illuminated in many books and videos about the "Law of Attraction," a "New Age" topic that has recently found popularity among mainstream audiences, celebrities, and even business professionals. The Law states that thoughts attract experiences that reinforce them, so that dwelling on negative circumstances can keep them in place, while focusing on positive experiences creates improved circumstances. Changing one's thoughts is harder than it might seem, of course, which is possibly why so much information and advice regarding the Law of Attraction is currently available.

The Hermetic Principle

Witchcraft can be said to employ the Law of Attraction in a sense, though magic can be much more complex than simply focusing one's thoughts on a desired outcome. It might be more accurate to say that Witches employ rituals, tools, words, and gifts from the natural world to enhance and expand their work with the Hermetic Principles, which are where the Law of Attraction comes from.

The Hermetic Principles date back to late antiquity and have informed Western religious, philosophical, esoteric and scientific thought. They have interesting parallels in modern physics, including quantum mechanics and string theory, and describe the way reality operates on a subatomic level, where all material things are composed of energy and radiate energy. Many Witches have been watching excitedly as the scientific understanding of the makeup of the Universe unfolds to confirm what ancient observers knew.

There are seven Hermetic Principles (also known as "Hermetic Laws"), which are often referred to in discussions of magic. One of the most emphasized is the Law of Correspondence, which states that what is true on the macrocosm is also true on the microcosm. This means that every particle of matter contains all others—and that linear time on the physical plane represents only one dimension in the ultimately spaceless and timeless overall Universe. Another way of stating the principle is "as above, so below; as below, so above." The higher planes of existence influence the lower planes of existence, and vice versa. As microcosms of the Universe, we are able to glean information from the distant past, view images of the future through divination, and change our reality.

A recent and widely-reported study found that the laws governing the growth of the Universe share significant similarities to the growth of both the human brain and the Internet. This is an interesting illustration of the Law of Correspondence, and also provides a window into the Law of Mentalism, another important principle of Witchcraft.

Just as every particle of matter contains all others, matter and energy all contain information at their most basic level. The Universe, ultimately, is mental at its highest level, which is the underlying creative force of all things. We know that all the inventions, developments, and adaptations in our human history began as ideas. Witches also know that thoughts can influence the Universal mind, and this is part of why focused intention in ritual is important.

The Law of Vibration holds that everything is in constant motion, and that nothing is at rest. This applies even to seemingly sturdy physical objects such as chairs and tables—they have vibrations than we simply can't perceive with the human mind. Matter is composed of energy, which is essentially a force moving at a certain vibration. The parallel with animism is worth noting here, as animists believe that everything is alive. If a characteristic of being "alive" is to be in motion, then the animists have been correct all along.

The nature of colors as light moving at different rates of vibration is particularly useful in Witchcraft, as each color's frequency has particular characteristics suitable for specific purposes. We often associate love with the colors red and pink, for example, and it turns out that these colors resonate with energies in the body that promote loving feelings. Therefore, these colors, when used in spellwork to bring love into one's life, both communicate that information to the Universe and connect it to the Witch's energy field. Of course, like all things, colors can have their down sides. The intense vibration of red can also overstimulate and trigger unpleasant feelings. Color therapies using the Chakra system and meditation techniques often seek to balance out-of-whack vibrations in the body, and colors can be used magically in much the same way.

Understanding systems like the Hermetic Principles and the Law of Attraction can be helpful in increasing one's success in magic, but a thorough grounding in them is not entirely necessary. And it's helpful to remember that no matter how powerful the intentions for magic may be, results may be limited by the endless unknown realities of the physical and higher planes—sometimes we're just not meant to get exactly what we want at a particular time. It may be that someone else would be harmed in some way, or that something else is already around the corner that will take care of our needs in a different way.

In fact, Witches can learn a lot about the nature of the Universe by observing which of their magical workings succeed, and which do not. The study of the Craft is considered by most to be a lifelong pursuit, with ongoing learning and refining of practices. The wisdom of ongoing study makes even more sense when considering the parallels between the growth of the Universe and the growth of the human brain. As more learning occurs, more magical techniques are invented and developed, and there's all the more to catch up on.

RITUAL AND SPELLWORK

It might be said that Wicca, as a religion, recognizes the laws of the Universe symbolically through the Goddess and God, the Wheel of the Year, and reverence for all living things.

Rituals performed in celebration of these aspects of the Universe may or may not involve magical work, as some Wiccans prefer to focus on what they view as the "spiritual" side of life. Witches, on the other hand, tend to blend ritual with magic, and may actually focus solely on working to transform reality for the benefit of themselves and others. This doesn't necessarily mean they don't consider themselves spiritual. Indeed, if all matter contains all matter, then there really is no separation between spiritual concerns and the concerns of everyday life.

Whether or not magic is being worked in a given ritual, Wiccans and other Witches tend to incorporate a few common structures in their formal activities, including casting a sacred or magical circle, invoking deities and/or particular powers using special words and phrases, and closing the circle at the end of the ritual. Movement, dance, chanting or singing may also be part of the activities.

These formal steps communicate to the higher realms of the Universe the thoughts and intentions of the practitioner(s) in a focused and effective manner, concentrating the energies of intention clearly and definitively. Energy, as physical matter, is raised in ritual and directed toward specific purposes, whether for gratitude and celebration, manifesting solutions to problems, or both.

Casting the Circle

As a symbol, the circle represents the Moon, the Earth, and the abundance of the Goddess. For this reason, a circle is able to safely contain the physical quantity of energy raised by the Witch or Witches performing the ritual, and see its transformation through to the higher realms. The circle is an infinitely portable tool, as it can be drawn anywhere, either physically or psychically, subtly or elaborately, depending on the circumstances.

The circle is as big or small as appropriate, but has to have enough room for the altar, everything being used in the ritual, and everyone participating—I'll be introducing to you the altar and ritual tools in the next section. It is usually marked on the floor of the space being used for ritual, often with sea salt first, followed by candles, or other magical items charged with energy for the purpose of ritual, such as crystals and semiprecious gemstones, or even herbs.

Once energy is raised inside the circle, the circle must remain closed until the end of the ritual. This keeps the energy from mingling with inappropriate or distracting energy from the rest of the physical plane, which strengthens the magic and protects practitioners from unwanted energetic interference.

No one can step outside of the circle while it is active without first performing an energetic manipulation, such as a "circle-cutting" spell, which creates an energetic "doorway" that is safe to exit and reenter. Once the circle is reentered, the door is closed and the circle reconnected.

Calling the Quarters

Also referred to as "drawing the quarters" this is a way of acknowledging the four cardinal directions and their Elemental associations, as well as the chosen deities of the coven or solitary Witch.

In a coven, either the High Priestess, the High Priest, or another coven member will walk around the circle, stopping in each cardinal direction to invoke the presence of its associated Element and, if applicable, god or goddess. (It should be remembered here that not all coven structures involve hierarchy—some covens simply have each member take turns performing this and any other necessary roles in ritual.) Specific words are usually spoken to invoke the specific powers and blessings of the element and/or deity being called. Once this is complete, the space is ready for the heart of the ritual.

Types of Ritual

The heart of the ritual may be a Sabbat or Esbat celebration, or it may celebrate a life event such as an initiation into a coven, a self-initiation for solitary and eclectic Witches, a handfasting (wedding), or an end of life ceremony. There are as many variations on each of these types of ritual as there are covens and solitary practitioners, and the way a particular Sabbat or Esbat is celebrated may morph and change over the years—in fact, many rituals are made up on the spot.

Furthermore, most covens don't share details of their rituals with non-members. All of this makes it difficult to generalize about the proceedings of ritual in Witchcraft. However, many examples are available in books about the Craft and on Wiccan and other Pagan websites.

At some point during the ritual, magical spells may be worked. Divination may also be employed, particularly at Samhain, though this might take place after the ritual as well. Once all of the ritual work is completed, the circle is closed, often in a reverse manner to the way it is opened, with the Witch thanking and dismissing the Elements and deities invoked at the start, while walking in the opposite direction. This ensures that the energy raised during ritual has gone completely to its destination in the higher realms, and is not squandered or neglected in the physical plane. It also helps ground the Witch(es) more firmly in the physical plane after reaching intense states of consciousness.

Magical Work

The types, forms, and intentions of magical work occurring during a Wiccan ritual are as varied as every other aspect of Wicca and Witchcraft: It may involve any combination of actions, tools, words, simple or complex spellwork, a tea or brew, chanting and/or movement, candle work, etc.

The options for magical discovery are truly endless. The purpose of the magic can also be anything under the sun—as long as the impact is positive, and does no harm. Many Wiccans choose to work for spiritual as well as material progress, using the Sabbats as opportunities to reflect on their lives at each point in the Wheel and work for balance or any desired change.

However, magical work does not have to be part of Wiccan ritual, and certainly isn't limited to it. Witches will incorporate magical work, as they are able and inclined to do so, into any part of their daily lives.

The tools described in the next section are used in both Wiccan ritual and many other forms of Witchcraft, in the ways and for the purposes that feel appropriate to the Witch(es) who use them.

THE TOOLS

Wiccans and other Witches incorporate a variety of objects into their rituals and magic, many of which are familiar to mainstream culture—you might have heard of some of these tools, and even be able to picture what they look like, from watching television and movies.

However, their presentation in the cinema is often incorrect, with more emphasis placed on entertainment, rather than being portraying the reality of a tool's usage and purpose. For this reason, many of the Wiccan tools are misunderstood.

Let's make this clear: Magic powers don't come streaming in a bolt of light from a Witch's wand, and no one flies on a broom. Both tools are important and sacred to Witchcraft, but in truth, a given Witch may use neither. This is because the power involved in Witchcraft is harnessed by Witches themselves—the tools are merely assistants.

Since the Universe is made of thought, it is ultimately the thought energy behind the actions performed with the tools that causes transformation of reality. Tools can be charged with magical energy, and can be very near and dear to the Witch, but they still need the Witch's intentions to work.

Broom

Perhaps the most common (and commonly misunderstood) symbol of Witches and Witchcraft in popular culture, the broom has been part of Wiccan and other pagan lore around the world for centuries. The sacred broom is not necessarily used in formal Wiccan ritual itself, but is often used to sweep energetic clutter from the ritual space beforehand. The bristles don't actually have to touch the ground, as this kind of cleansing is happening on the psychic and energetic level.

Because it serves as a purifier, it is associated with the element of Water, and is sacred to the Goddess. The broom can also be placed near the entrance to a home to guard against negative or unwanted energy.

The broom can be any size, from miniature "decorative" brooms to larger, full-sized brooms. It might even be a tree-branch used symbolically as a broom. Traditional woods used for sacred brooms include birch, ash, and willow. Many Witches keep hand-made brooms for ritual purposes, but a common household broom can also be dedicated to the work of Witchcraft. No matter what type or material, however, the ritual broom is never used for everyday housecleaning, as this would contaminate the sacred energy it holds for ritual and magical purposes.

Altar

The altar is the sacred place where tools are placed during Wiccan ritual and magic. Traditionally, the altar stands in the center of the circle of energy raised by the participant(s) in the ritual. It may be a table or other object with a flat surface, such as an old chest. It can be square or round, according to preference. Witches may decorate the altar with colored scarves or other material corresponding with the season or the particular purpose of the ritual.

Ideally, the altar is made of wood, such as oak, which is considered to hold significant power, or willow, which is considered sacred to the Goddess. However, it can really be made of any material, as any physical object charged with magical energy will contribute power to the ritual work being enacted.

Witches performing outdoor rituals may use an old tree stump, large stone, or other natural object for an altar, or may use a fire in place of the altar, placing the ritual tools elsewhere in the charged space.

While the altar is usually set up prior to the ritual and taken down afterward, some Witches maintain permanent altars in their homes. These may double as shrines to the Goddess and God, and can be a place to store the Witch's magical tools.

The tools are deliberately placed in specific patterns on the altar, with intentional regard to the elements and the four directions. For example, tools and symbols associated with the element of Earth may be placed in the North section of the altar, while those associated with water will be placed to the East. Traditional Wiccan practice also often devotes the left side of the altar to representations of the Goddess, while the right side represents the God. While many Witches closely follow established patterns for setting up the altar, others will experiment and use patterns that resonate with their personal relationship with their deities and corresponding tools and symbols.

Wand

Used for millennia in religious and magical rites, the wand has long been associated with Witches and Witchcraft in popular culture, and has also been quite misunderstood.

As with all magical tools, it is not the wand that causes magical transformation, but the Witch, who energetically charges the wand with magical intention. As a shape it takes the form of a line, and so is used to direct energy. It is often used in Wiccan ritual to invoke the Goddess and God, and may be used to draw magical symbols in the air or on the ground. It can also be used to draw the circle within which the ritual or spellwork is performed. The wand is associated with the element of Air, and is considered sacred to the God.

The wand can be a fairly simple affair, simply cut from a slight branch or twig from a tree (with an attitude of reverence and respect for the tree making the sacrifice). Generally, the wand isn't much longer than the forearm, and can be shorter. Woods traditionally used to make the wand include oak, willow, elder, and hazel. Witches without access to these or other trees might purchase a wooden dowel from a craft or hardware store to decorate and consecrate as a wand. There are also a number of very fancy glass or pewter-based wands decorated with engravings and crystals available at many New Age stores, but wood is the traditional material for Wiccan wands, and it is generally thought that a wand *made* by the Witch who uses it is more effective.

Knife

Also called an *athame*, the ritual knife, like the wand, is a tool that directs energy in ritual, and may also be used to draw the circle before ritual and close the circle afterward.

However, it is more of an energy manipulator or commander, due to its sharp edges, and therefore isn't generally used to invoke deities, as this would be considered forceful, rather than collaborative, in terms of working with divine energy. The athame is also used to draw magical symbols, such as the pentagram, in the air to lend power to ritual and spellwork, and is often employed in rituals that banish and/or release negative energies or influences. This tool is associated with the God, and the element of Fire, as it is an agent that causes change.

The knife is traditionally sharp on both sides, with a black handle which is said to store a small amount of the magical energy raised in rituals for later use. The blade is not generally very long—the length of one's hand, or shorter, is considered ideal.

Some Witches purchase special daggers to serve as their athame, while others will consecrate an ordinary kitchen knife for the purpose. It's considered unwise to use a knife that has been used to cut animal flesh, though any negative energies lingering from such use can be ritually cleansed before "converting" the knife into an athame. Some Witches choose to enhance their energetic relationship with their knife by engraving magical symbols into the handle.

Depending on the tradition, the athame may do double duty as an actual cutting and engraving tool. It may be used to cut herbs, shape a new wand from the branch of a tree, or carve magical symbols into a candle for ritual use. However, many Witches prefer to use a second, white-handled knife (sometimes called a *boline*) for these purposes, keeping the athame for ritual use only.

Cauldron

While the word "cauldron" may bring to mind images of Shakespeare's three witches tossing all kinds of animal parts into a boiling stew for evil purposes, the cauldron is really a symbol of the Goddess and the creative forces of transformation. Cauldrons appear in many ancient Celtic myths in connection with magical occurrences, and continue to influence Witchcraft today. Associated with the element of Water, the cauldron may hold magically charged ingredients for a potion, or may be used to allow spell candles to burn out. It can also be filled with fresh water and used for scrying.

Cast iron is considered the cauldron's ideal material, though other metals are often used. Most rest on three legs, with the opening of the cauldron having a smaller diameter than the widest part of the bowl. Cauldrons can be anywhere from a few inches to a few feet across in diameter, though larger sizes may be considered impractical. While some Witches may actually brew a magical potion right in the cauldron, the practical constraints of lighting a safe indoor fire underneath it tend to limit this use—often, the "brewing" aspect of the magic is symbolic rather than literal.

Cup

Like the cauldron, the cup represents the element of Water and symbolizes the fertility of the Goddess.

An important element of the altar layout during ritual, it may hold water, wine, or possibly a special tea brewed for the magical purpose of the rite. In some rituals it remains empty, as a symbol of readiness to receive new sources of abundance from the Spirit world. Also called the "goblet" or the "chalice" in some traditions, it can be made of any quality substance such as earthenware, crystal, glass, or silver. Solitary Witches may simply dedicate a favorite old family cup, charging it with magical energy and keeping it just for this purpose.

Pentacle

The pentacle is an important symbol-bearer in Witchcraft, normally inscribed with a pentagram, though other magical symbols may be present. The pentagram itself is a five-pointed star, drawn with five straight lines, often encircled, and always having one upward point. Each point is said to represent the elements of Air, Earth, Fire, and Water, with the Fifth Element (Spirit) as the upward point.

As a symbol, it is found in both ancient Eastern and Western cultures and has been used to represent various aspects of human and spiritual concerns. The pentagram is considered to have inherent magical powers, and is often inscribed on objects as well as in the air during rituals, to add strength to the work. It is also considered a sign of protection from negative or harmful energies.

As a bearer of this Earth-related symbol, the pentacle is used to consecrate other tools and objects used in ritual. Usually a flat, round piece of wood, clay, wax, or silver, it can be any size, though generally is small enough to fit comfortably on the altar with the other tools. The pentacle may be ornately carved and/or set with semiprecious gemstones, or may be a simple design. Witches may also wear a pentacle on a cord or chain during ritual, or even as part of their daily dress, though they may or may not choose to wear it publicly.

Incense

Incense is associated with the element of Air, and, in some traditions, Fire. Smoldering incense is often placed before images of the deities on an altar or a shrine. Many Witches feel that incense is an essential component to successful ritual. This is partly due to the consciousness-altering potential of quality incense, which can facilitate a more focused state of mind when performing magical work.

Smoke from the incense can also provide visions of the deities being invoked in ritual, or other images pertinent to the work being performed. Furthermore, certain herbs, spices, barks, and roots have specific magical qualities, so homemade incense blends can be used to strengthen magical spells.

Whether homemade or store-bought, traditional Wiccan rituals favor raw or granulated incense, which requires charcoal briquettes to burn on, and is usually held in a censer. The censer can be a traditional swinging censer suspended from chains, like those used in the Catholic church, or a more simple construction, depending on whether the incense is moved around during the ritual. Some Witches may let the incense smolder in the cauldron in lieu of a censer.

For Witches who are more sensitive to incense smoke, lighter stick or cone incenses may work better. Some opt for scenting their magical candles with oils instead. Whatever the choice, it's generally agreed that some form of aromatic enhancement is optimal for magical work.

Crystals, Stones, Herbs, and Oils

Perhaps some of the most powerful magical tools are those that come straight from the Earth without much, if any, alteration by human hands. Herbs and semiprecious gemstones have long been known to have healing properties, and are used today in many medicinal systems around the globe. They are also used in Witchcraft, as decorations, offerings, magical enhancements, and even as the focus of some rituals and spells.

Crystals and other stones have their own energies and are considered to be "alive," rather than simply dormant matter. Sensitive people can often feel their energies when holding these stones in their hands or on some other part of their bodies.

Some stones are used for specific purposes in ritual, while others may be more permanent presences on the altar or in other places in a Witch's home. They may range in size from a square half-inch to much larger, and may be polished and/or carved into specific shapes, or left in their raw form. Crystals can be found in many New Age stores as well as online, though they can sometimes still be found in their raw form in certain natural areas.

Crystals may be used to help guard against illness or negative energy, or may aid in divination or other psychic work. They may also be used to lay out the magic circle at the start of ritual. These stones have astrological associations as well as associations with specific gods and goddesses.

Herbs are also associated with specific deities and astrological bodies, and are used in a variety of ways, including magical kitchen edibles, brews and potions, and spell ingredients. Some of the most common kitchen herbs, such as basil, rosemary, and thyme also have magical associations, which doubles their potential for effective magic, as they can be used to make "enchanted" foods.

However, other herbs used in magic are not appropriate to consume, and care should always be taken to know the difference. It is considered ideal for Witches to harvest their own herbs with their ritual knives, whether from a nearby woods or their own kitchen herb "gardens." However, fresh herbs can be found in grocery stores, and many natural food stores also sell a variety of dried herbs in their bulk departments.

Essential oils from plants, seeds, and nuts are used to enhance ritual atmosphere and also as ingredients in spellwork. Oils have metaphysical properties and may be rubbed into spell candles for a specific magical purpose, or used in a skin-safe blend to anoint the body before ritual. Witches often make their own blends of essential oils to strengthen ritual and spellwork. Also used in aromatherapy for healing a number of physical and emotional ailments, essential oils are widely available at natural food stores.

Candles

Last but certainly not least, candles are considered essential to the practice of Witchcraft.

Used as a source of light, as devotional symbols of deity, as a means of communicating with Spirit, and to aid transformation in many spells, candles have a magical way about them as they allow us to work directly with the element of Fire.

Witches work with a variety of candle colors, depending on the deities being represented and/or invoked, as well as any particular magical purposes of a ritual or spell. Candles are a simple and direct way to work with color magic. Colors have their own metaphysical properties, as well as astrological and elemental associations, which will be described in the next section of this guide.

Candles used in the Craft do not need to be fancy or expensive, though some Witches like to have one or more large, long-lasting candles for use on the altar. Candles used for specific spell purposes are usually left to burn out on their own, and so for practical reasons tend to be smaller. Beeswax, tapers, votives and tea light candles can all be used, though many shops sell individual candles sized and colored specifically for spellwork. These tend to be no more than 4 inches tall and less than one half-inch in diameter.

Witches will generally distinguish between candles used for specific ritual purposes and more "multi-purpose" candles used for additional lighting during spellwork (or simply to enhance any evening atmosphere). Candles consecrated for magical use are therefore not used for any other purposes.

Other Tools

Depending on the tradition, the coven, and/or the individual Witch, variations and additions to the tools described above may be used in ritual and spellwork. For example, some Witches use a sword in addition to, or in place of, the ritual knife. However, swords can be impractical for indoor ritual due to their size, and are not as easily obtainable as knives, and so are less commonly used.

A staff is also sometimes used in formal ritual, held by the High Priest or Priestess of a coven. Like the wand, it carries the representations of Air and the God, though in some traditions it represents Fire. It is usually made of wood and may be decorated with magical symbols and/or semiprecious stones.

Many Witches also incorporate divination tools in their ritual practice. These may include runes, tarot cards, a quartz crystal sphere (or "crystal ball") for scrying, or other oracles borrowed from older traditions, such as the I-Ching. Individual items, such as a specific Tarot card or rune, may be incorporated into spells for specific purposes. The crystal sphere is often used on the altar to represent the Goddess. As mentioned previously, divination may take place during a formal ritual, but post-ritual is also considered a good time for this activity, as the Witch is still in a conducive state of mind to communicate with the Spirit world at this time.

Finally, many Witches like to include magically charged jewelry and other elements of "costume" into their practice. Some may simply wear a pentacle on a chain, as mentioned above, while others may don special robes and/or a headpiece encrusted with gemstones to enhance their personal energy during ritual. Witches in some traditions also work naked, which is generally referred to as "sky-clad."

As with any other aspect of Wicca and Witchcraft, there is no set-in-stone way to approach using the tools of ritual and magic. While it's generally considered helpful to use at least a few, if not several, of the tools described above, it is ultimately about the Witch and his or her connection to the specific tools chosen, or the coven members' collective affinities for the specifics of their ritual practice. Those identifying as Wiccans are likely to have some symbolic representation of the Goddess and God at Sabbat celebrations, and the Goddess at Esbats, but the way this is carried out can vary widely.

While some covens and solitaries may create elaborate rituals using every tool imaginable, others may design very simple affairs involving simply a candle and a crystal. In other words, it's more about using what *feels* inspiring and "in tune," rather than gathering items from a checklist—if it feels out of place, or unpleasantly strange to a particular Witch to purchase and use a cauldron or a censer, or wear special robes, then these items may simply not be necessary or suitable for that person.

This is, of course, a very brief overview of the basic concepts, forms and tools involved in Wicca and other Witchcraft, as opposed to a comprehensive discussion—as is to be expected with such an unusual and widely varying religion as Wicca, other sources will have different things to say about many of the topics discussed here. Readers interested in learning more should consult as many references as they please for a deeper understanding of these beliefs and practices.

For those considering adopting any or all of the practices discussed in this guide, the next section will explore several practical steps one can take on their journey towards practicing Wicca.

PART THREE

NEXT STEPS FOR ASPIRING WICCANS

MOVING FORWARD

Wicca is different from other religions in many respects, not least of which is its lack of centralized structure and official, authoritative texts that spell out specific forms of practice for all to follow.

It also doesn't tend to be evangelistic or seek new members—you won't find many fliers or posters inviting you to the next Sabbat celebration with your local coven.

This leaves it up to individuals interested in the Craft to seek out information and possible connections with others in the Wiccan community. Thankfully, the Internet has made it far easier than it used to be for Wiccans and Witches to find and post information and communicate with each other.

READ AND REACH OUT

The best way to get started is to read widely about Wicca and/or other forms of Paganism. A short list of suggested references is at the end of this guide, and there is an enormous variety of information available in bookstores and online, much of it from venerable and experienced sources. New voices with new visions for the Craft also continue to emerge.

If you read widely enough, you'll encounter conflicting beliefs and advice—and this is a good thing, as it allows you to develop your own personal understanding of the forces and phenomena at work in Wicca and Witchcraft. Follow what resonates with you at the deepest level. If a ritual, spell, a particular philosophy or any other idea doesn't appeal to you, leave it out of your developing practice and keep seeking more information that feels "right." Most Wiccans and Witches will tell you that it takes a long time of study and observation to create an authentic personal relationship with the Craft.

If you're looking to connect with others, depending on where you live there may in fact be a local coven, circle, or other such group that you could join, or at least approach for information and advice. If there is a spiritual or "New Age" store in your area, odds are that someone there will know of any existing groups. You can also check event listings online, in local newspapers, or other community resources. Finally, you can send out an intention to the Universe to help bring the people you're looking for into your life—it may be that a group near you is looking for someone new to join and will look forward to receiving your message!

You can also always start your own "study group" to find like-minded souls who also want to learn more about Wicca, Witchcraft, and/or other forms of Paganism.

COVEN, CIRCLE, SOLITARY, OR ECLECTIC?

For those interested in working with other Wiccans and Witches, covens and circles can be a good way to get solid training and advice from experienced practitioners. The terms "coven" and "circle" *can* be confusing for beginners, as they often seem to be used interchangeably. They are not, however, the same thing.

A *circle* is usually a fairly informal group whose members may get together to discuss and learn about the Craft, and may experiment with different kinds of ritual and spellwork. They may or may not meet for Sabbats and/or Esbats, depending on the collective wishes of the group. Depending on how "open" the group is, there may be many members, some of whom drop in and out as it suits them, or just a few regularly involved friends. The structure of a circle is generally loose and doesn't require official initiation or involve an established hierarchy.

A *coven,* on the other hand, is more structured and usually has one or more established leaders, such as a High Priestess and/or High Priest, especially in what is referred to as "Traditional" Wicca. Covens meet for Sabbats and Esbats and members are expected to attend these gatherings, as the participation of each person is important to the ritual. Initiation is generally required, though it's fairly unlikely that someone brand-new to Wicca will be quickly initiated into a coven, for a few reasons.

One is that covens are generally small groups, with seven being considered an ideal number, and there's a tradition of not going over 13 members—often, if there's enough interest to push a coven past 13, one member will depart to start a new, separate coven. So, depending on how well established a coven is, there may just simply not be any openings.

Secondly, coven members will want potential new initiates to have spent a good deal of time studying before considering inviting them to participate in formal ritual.

Finally, since the bonds formed between coven members are strong and fairly intimate, the question of whether someone's personality and general energy are a good fit is an important one.

For those who don't live near any covens or circles, or who simply prefer not to incorporate a social element into their experience of the Craft, the life of a solitary or eclectic Witch can be just as meaningful and rewarding. Perhaps you'd rather get to know the spiritual and magical dimensions of the Universe on your own for awhile, and then consider reaching out to like-minded others, or perhaps you're just born to be a solo practitioner—and that's perfectly fine! No matter which direction you choose, there's a plethora of informational sources out there to guide you along the way.

The terms "solitary" and "eclectic" may sometimes be used interchangeably, as there can be a lot of overlap, but the distinctions are worth pointing out here.

"*Solitary*" refers to the practice of Wicca or Witchcraft on one's own, without any group experience such as a coven or circle. Wiccans who belong to covens may (and often do) still practice on their own along with their participation in coven work, but a solitary Wiccan or Witch *always* works alone.

A solitary Witch can still intentionally follow what is commonly agreed to be "Traditional" Wicca, such as Gardnerian, British Traditional Wicca, or another "lineage-based" tradition, and those who do so tend to identify as "solitary" rather than "eclectic."

"*Eclectic*" is a description for Witches who don't follow a single, specific tradition and instead borrow and blend ideas, methods, practices, etc. from a variety of sources, and may also (and often do) invent their own. Some covens also consider themselves to be "eclectic," although this tends to irritate members of traditional covens.

It's worth remembering here that even the earliest recognized forms of Traditional Wicca were essentially borrowed, blended, and "invented" themselves.

FINDING YOUR WAY IN

In this section, I want to show you how a newcomer to Wicca may begin to embrace the Wiccan beliefs, way of life, and rituals.

Living the Wheel of the Year

Wicca and Witchcraft are rooted in a relationship with nature and its various expressions in plant and animal life, the elements, and the turning of the seasons. The living, breathing Divine Mind is vibrantly present in nature, perhaps more obviously so than in most of the human-made, modern, "developed world." Those interested in Wicca and Witchcraft will benefit from consciously observing the natural world around them and developing a more intentional relationship with it.

Witches who live in climates with four distinct seasons (Spring, Summer, Autumn and Winter) have an excellent opportunity to closely observe the Wheel of the Year. Sabbats are the best time to note the changes on the Earth and in the sky over the last several weeks, and Esbats also provide occasions for marking the seasons' effects in our everyday lives. The more you pay attention to the space "in between seasons," the more the movement of the Earth becomes apparent—even in Winter.

If you live in a climate with less seasonal variety, or even none at all to speak of, you can still observe the effects of natural forces in subtle ways. The sun still casts different qualities of light throughout the day. The air tends to change just before a rain. Becoming practiced in the habit of observing small details in your natural environment helps cultivate your openness to the unseen energies inherent in all of the Universe.

If you can, go out for walks, hikes, picnics, etc. in places with soil and vegetation. Or go swimming, canoeing, or rock-skipping across a pond. Build a snowman or sculpt your own creation in snow. Do whatever you can to spend some quality time outdoors on a regular basis.

If you live in a very urban environment and have little in the way of access to natural areas, you can still create ways to interact with the underlying forces of the Universe. Parks can be suitable, but so can indoor plants and windowsill gardens. You can grow herbs for magical use and healing as well as cooking. Open a window at sunrise and study whatever you can see of the sky. Stand in the rain for a minute and embrace the feeling of it on your skin. Even nature shows and photographs or art depicting natural scenes can help put you in touch, as well as recordings of nature sounds and meditation music.

When Sabbats come around, make a point of gathering a few of the seasonal gifts of the Earth—flower petals in Spring months, leaves shed from deciduous trees in Autumn, pine needles from evergreens in Winter. Use these in ritual, or simply as decorations on your kitchen table or somewhere else where you'll see them often. As you practice these ways of observing the Wheel of the Year, you'll find your relationship with the seasons (even your least favorite ones) becoming more attuned and rooted in gratitude.

Deities and the Divine

Seeking and attaining a spiritual relationship with the Triple Goddess or Cernunnos or Diana or any other number of deities from around the ancient world can be a very effective way into the Craft, and many people find their experience to be deepened and sharpened through the practice of more traditional, structured forms of Wicca.

But some newcomers to Wicca and Witchcraft are unsure about the notion of "worshipping" deities, and may feel strange about searching for one or more specific gods or goddesses to form relationships or alignments with. Borrowing from older traditions in this respect may not quite feel like an authentic approach to a spiritual search.

It's true that it takes time to find and cultivate an interest in and a relationship with a deity you weren't aware of until recently, and people who were raised in monotheistic religions can struggle even more with integrating the concept of polytheism. But it's also true that you don't absolutely *have* to incorporate a belief in or a relationship with any specific form of the divine. You might just work with the idea of a Goddess and a God, or even less definitively identified energies of the Universe.

Faith and belief are far more often developed and cultivated over time than immediately attained. Make effort to study and seek yours, but go at your own pace, and trust your intuition. No one can tell you you're not a true Wiccan or Witch because your relationship with the divine doesn't match their experience. (Well, some might, but in a religion with so many variations, it's only natural that some will quibble about the details.) There's no intermediary between you and the Universe, and there are as many paths to the Divine as there are people who seek it.

If you do see connecting with deities as a possible part of your path, start doing some research. Read about them—in Wiccan books, in ancient myths, in poetry, in history books. (Watch out for bias in the history books, however—in the Judeo-Christian world, the deities of polytheism often get negatively and erroneously portrayed.) You may discover, as some Witches do, that a deity will actually find you, through images, dreams, seemingly "random" events or coincidences, or in other ways.

Meditation and Visualization

Preparing for ritual and magical work involves accessing a beneficial altered state of mind that allows for both openness and focus. Many traditions practice specific meditation and visualization techniques to strengthen this ability and call on it when needed. You can find information on meditation in Witchcraft or many other spiritual traditions. Seek out different kinds of meditation instruction and practice what works best for you. If nothing else, be sure to set aside time and space for solitude and reflection, preferably every day, but definitely before ritual and spellwork.

EXAMPLE SPELL: A RITUAL OF CELEBRATION AND MAGIC FOR THE AUTUMN EQUINOX

This fairly simple ritual is offered as one example of countless possibilities—I've included it to show you an example of one of the more accessible, and easy-to-perform rituals for the beginner Wiccan.

It's designed for solitary practice, but could certainly be adapted for use with a coven. Like most rituals, it can be tailored to your intuition, preferences, or circumstances. (It can also be replicated for other Sabbats, with changes made to seasonal items, candle colors, etc.) If you don't have everything listed below, you don't have to go out and buy it—you can substitute, simplify, and improvise as you wish. However, you should at least have a candle or two, and some form of recognition of the season to serve as points of focus for your energy—remember, most of the tools are symbolic as the power comes from you, but tools are especially useful for beginners as they give them something tangible to focus and direct their energy onto.

Ready to get started?

Since the Autumn Equinox is a time for celebrating the abundance of the harvest, themes for focus in ritual include gratitude to the Sun for making the harvest possible and to the Earth for yielding abundance to carry through the Winter months.

The balance of equal day and equal night is also good to observe, as is the opportunity to begin a turning inward and looking forward to a more restful time. The end of Summer is also a time when the abundance of the Earth begins to die back in order to make room for new growth in the next cycle. We can use this time to identify what in our lives isn't needed anymore—whether it be too much "stuff," an old habit we've been wanting to break, or anything else that we'd like to release back into the Universe.

As you prepare for the ritual, meditate on these themes and notice what comes to mind. See this opportunity to gain insight into an aspect of your life you may not have been conscious of before.

Recommended Items

- Seasonal representations such as late summer crops, especially corn and squash, apples, seeds, and/or marigolds.

- Candles: 1 black, 1 white, 1 dark green spell candle, and 1 or more others in autumn colors like red, orange, brown, gold, etc.

- Pentacle

- Cup

- Incense and/or oils: frankincense, sandalwood, pine, rosemary, chamomile

- Stones: jade, carnelian, lapis lazuli

- Herbs: sage, hawthorne, cedar

Instructions

Lay out your tools on your altar or ritual space. You can do this in whatever way is most visually pleasing, or you can follow any traditional pattern that appeals to you.

One way is to place the white candle on the left for the Goddess, the black candle on the right for the God, the pentacle to the North and the cup to the West. A candle can be placed in the South—this can be the spell candle, if you're using it, or another candle. Incense or oils can be placed in the East. (If it's not practical to place burning incense right on the altar, you can place it somewhere nearby in the Eastern quarter.) Any stones or representations of the harvest can be placed around the edges of the altar or wherever they seem to "want" to be. Take some time trying out different arrangements. You'll soon get a sense for what looks and feels right for you.

If you want to cast a circle, make sure you have everything you're using for the ritual, and then decide how large your circle will need to be. Using sea salt, sprinkled herbs, candles, or stones, mark out the circle on the ground. Charge the circle with intention for creating a sacred space by slowly walking clockwise around it from the inside. As you walk, "draw" the circle again by pointing with your index finger, visualizing the energetic connection between your body and the circle's edge—remember, you are creating a place of higher, more powerful energy than will exist on the outside of the circle. This is an act that takes practice and learning. It is not strictly necessary, but it is a time-honored part of Wiccan tradition that many find to be integral.

Light the black and white candles and invite the God and Goddess (or the balanced forces of male and female) to be present with you in the celebration. If you wish, call the quarters by turning to stand in each cardinal direction, starting with North and moving clockwise. Verbally recognize each direction by name and its associated element, and ask for its energy to come into your circle. You are already incorporating symbols of the Elements with the pentacle (Earth), the incense or oil (Air), the candles (Fire), and the cup (Water) so you could hold each of these items as you greet the Elements, either instead of calling the quarters or as part of it.

Reflect on the abundance you've experienced in the past season. Identify 7 things you are grateful for and state them aloud. These can be small things or larger ones—whatever you feel truly grateful for at this time. Then, ask for any help you need with establishing balance, maintaining security, and/or letting go of something.

If you're using a spell candle, rub a drop or two of essential oil into it, or just hold it in your hands for a few moments. Visualize yourself feeling secure and grateful for abundance in your life, in good physical health, and emotionally balanced. Out loud, state this vision in whatever way seems most natural to you. You might simply say "I have everything I need. I am in good health. My life is balanced."

Light the green candle as you say the words. Then "seal" the work with a final phrase. Many Witches use one of the following: "So let it be," "So mote it be," "Blessed Be," or "It is done." Whatever you choose, be sure to consciously release your intentions into the higher realms where they can be transformed and manifest. Watch the flame for a few moments, feeling the positive energies raised within you and all around you in the sacred space.

When you're ready, thank the Elements, then the Goddess and God for their presence. Then, close the circle by walking around it counter-clockwise, releasing its energy into the Universe. (Note: Don't leave any candles unattended, but do let the spell candle burn out on its own, if at all possible.)

Over the next few weeks, continue the practice of recognizing abundance and expressing gratitude. You may also notice any seeming imbalances in your life or well-being and decide to do what you can to correct them. If you do so, you will see that the Universe will support you!

WHAT DOES MANIFESTATION LOOK LIKE?

When Witches speak of "manifestation" or "success" in relation to prayer, intention, or spellwork, what do they really mean?

You don't tend to hear fairytale-like stories about enormous, overnight gains in one's quality of life the day after working a spell, though anything can happen if all the right circumstances are in place. What advanced practitioners of the Craft understand is that *practice* is necessary—in the form of time, study, and experiment. One also has to cultivate a mindset that is open to manifestation, to success, and to magical and positive occurrences.

This *can* be a difficult habit to acquire and hold onto, and everyone has their blind spots now and again, but with active practice, the wonders of the Universe begin to unfold more steadily.

Let me show you how.

Once upon a time, a young, aspiring Witch met an older, much more experienced Witch at a folk festival, where they were both camping in the woods. As the festival wound down and everyone was packing up to leave, the two Witches decided to exchange their contact information. Neither had a writing implement, nor could they find any in their tents or packs. Then suddenly, the younger Witch spotted a pencil, "randomly" lying on the forest floor between two trees. "Wow," said the older Witch. "Talk about manifesting!"

The younger Witch was confused. How was this an example of "manifesting"? The pencil hadn't fallen from the sky, or even been suddenly delivered by a passerby out of the blue. Sure, it was a welcome coincidence, but clearly some other person had simply lost a pencil in that spot in the woods, and over a festival weekend, those woods saw their fair share of human artifacts. Furthermore, no spell or incantation had been performed. So how did this pencil count as a manifestation?

The younger Witch was too accustomed to analyzing the possible causes of events to appreciate the synchronicity and Divine timing of this pencil's emergence into her reality. Rather than focusing on the inherent magic of this small event, she instinctively moved to dismiss it in favor of the habitual "rational" thinking instilled in her through cultural conditioning.

This is a challenge faced by many who are new to the Craft, but with persistent willingness to be open to the subtleties of reality underneath our "rational" experience, it becomes easier to recognize all kinds of manifestations, from the "little things" to much larger transformations in our lives.

There are a few key elements in this particular incident that meet the conceptual requirements of manifestation. First, the pencil appeared in the right place at the right time. Second, it fulfilled a specific need that, if met, would be beneficial to both people involved, and would harm no one. Third, it happened in a way that was unexpected, rather than as a result of looking in all the obvious, logical places for something to write with. Manifestation often comes in ways we never could have imagined or planned for.

And as an extra-nice touch, it happened in a natural setting: a forest of old, magnificent trees.

Just as importantly, the pencil was *acknowledged* as a manifestation by the older Witch, who knew from practice how to recognize and appreciate it as such. She also knew that manifestation can happen with or without designated spellwork. Sometimes the Universe simply helps out in moments of need or crisis—these occasions are sometimes called "miracles." Since the older Witch was well grounded in magical principles, she was often able to intend for things immediately and did so habitually, always growing in her ability to connect her personal power with the Divine.

Beyond spellwork, ritual, and intention-setting, the practice of paying attention and acknowledging with gratitude is just as important to successful manifestation. As you start seeing synchronicities in your life, however small, take note and remember them. You may want to record incidents that seem significant in a journal or Book of Shadows. You will find that the more you pay attention to them, the more you will attract positive manifestation in your life.

KEEPING A BOOK OF SHADOWS

The term "Book of Shadows" comes out of the Gardnerian Tradition, but has been widely adopted and adapted by covens, solitaries, and eclectics ever since. Keeping one is a great way for new and experienced Witches alike to deepen their practice of the Craft.

You can think of your Book of Shadows as a kind of journal, specifically for spiritual and/or magical pursuits. The contents of a Book of Shadows are personal and will vary from Witch to Witch. Some keep detailed instructions for rituals and spells, either borrowed from other sources or of their own invention. Some record the results of their magical workings, information about their personal deity alignments, or lists of particular herbs and stones they feel affinity with. Others may free-write about their intentions for a coming ritual or a new season. This can also be a good place to record relevant dreams or other signs and messages that come into your life. It's often illuminating to revisit these at a later date and see underlying connections between seemingly unrelated phenomena!

These are just a few suggestions for digging deeper into the world of Wicca and Witchcraft. As we've seen, it's a wide and richly diverse religion with many possible avenues to follow. No matter what you do, always follow your own intuition when it comes to how, when, and if you want to embark on the path of the Craft.

CONCLUSION

Unlike most other Western religions, Wicca is highly decentralized—there is no official sacred text, no central governing body, and this means there is no one way to practice the religion.

With this in mind, it is very difficult to create a truly encompassing beginner's guide to the topic, simply because different Wiccans will interpret the many facets of the religion differently—in some cases, *very* differently.

In this guide, I have tried to provide an unbiased approach, though undoubtedly my own experiences as a practicing Wiccan might have influenced certain sections of this book. Generally speaking, I have tried to include the most *"popular"* approach to each topic, as this should make the information easier to digest, and you are also more likely to encounter Wiccans with the same set of beliefs—this might make it easier for you to find a local coven with a set of beliefs that truly resonate with you.

However, nothing in this inspiring, fascinating religion is set in stone. Certain sections of this guide might not *feel* right to you, and that's perfectly fine. The great thing about Wicca is that you are free to come up with your own belief system, and as you meet and interact with fellow practitioners, you'll see that some people's interpretations might vary wildly from the views presented in this guide.

There is no right or wrong. As long as you keep the Wiccan principles at heart, and never intentionally seek to harm others, you can practice Wicca in any way you see fit. In fact, I would actively *encourage* you to seek out your own path.

One of the best things about Wicca is that your interpretations, views, and beliefs are highly flexible. When you are just starting out, you are encouraged to read and learn as much as possible, and so your initial beliefs are bound to be shaped by the guides you read.

Over time, when you begin to embrace Wicca in your daily life, you might have certain epiphanies that re-shape your approach to the practicing this religion. What you believe on day one, might be *very* different to your beliefs on day 100, which could be a world apart from your views on day 1,000. It can be a lifelong journey, and even after decades you will still find yourself learning new things. This is one of the many benefits of keeping your own Book of Shadows—you can literally track how your Wiccan journey has evolved over time.

Remember: nobody can tell you how to practice Wicca, and the religion can mean anything you want it to mean to you. While I have presented the information in this guide as "correct", I am in no way suggesting that it is the only way to practice Wicca. If you read other guides, there may be conflicting information. And when you read another guide to the topic, you will likely come across even more conflicting information!

That's just the way Wicca is. Even if you encounter some different opinions—even those completely opposed to what you have read in this guide!—it doesn't mean one guide is right, and another is wrong: it just means the many different authors have interpreted different aspects of the religion differently.

I will leave you with that thought, as it is now time for you to start your own journey, and interpret the information presented to you in your own way. I have included a number of tables of correspondence at the end of this guide, which you should find helpful at some point in time. I have also included a number of suggested sources for further reading, as in the early days it is important for you to absorb as much information as possible on the subject.

Thank you for reading, and good luck on your journey.

Blessed Be.

TABLES OF CORRESPONDENCE

Tables of correspondence illustrate various qualities and associations of tangible objects like crystals and stones, herbs, and oils, as well as intangible phenomena like colors, months, astrological signs, and even days of the week.

Included here are very brief sample tables of correspondence. You can consult these when exploring options for ritual, spellwork, and other Craft activity. Be sure to research further, however—there are countless tables of correspondence with much more detailed information than is presented in this brief guide.

TABLE ONE: COLORS

Color	Qualities	Magical Uses	Elemental and Other Associations
Red	Passion, courage, strength, intense emotions	Love, physical energy, health, willpower	Fire, South, Mars, Aries
Orange	Energy, attraction, vitality, stimulation	Adaptability to sudden changes, encouragement, power	Mercury, Gemini
Yellow	Intellect, inspiration, imagination, knowledge	Communication, confidence, divination, study	Air, East, Sun, Leo
Green	Abundance, growth, wealth, renewal, balance	Prosperity, employment, fertility, health, good luck	Earth, North, Venus, Libra & Taurus
Blue	Peace, truth, wisdom, protection, patience	Healing, psychic ability, harmony in the home, understanding	Water, West, Jupiter, Sagittarius

Color	Qualities	Magical Uses	Elemental and Other Associations
Indigo	Emotion, fluidity, insight, expressiveness	Meditation, clarity of purpose, spiritual healing, self-mastery	Saturn & Neptune, Capricorn & Pisces
Violet	Spirituality, wisdom, devotion, peace, idealism	Divination, enhancing nurturing qualities, balancing sensitivity	Uranus & Moon, Aquarius & Cancer
Black	Dignity, force, stability, protection	Banishing and releasing negative energies, transformation, enlightenment	Saturn & Pluto, Capricorn & Scorpio
White	Peace, innocence, illumination, purity	Cleansing, clarity, establishing order, spiritual growth and understanding	Spirit (the fifth Element), Mercury & Moon, Virgo

TABLE TWO:
CRYSTALS AND GEMSTONES

Crystal	Color(s)	Magical Uses
Amethyst	Violet	Sharpens mental focus and intuition, clears sacred spaces
Bloodstone	Green with flecks of red/gold	Promotes physical healing, fertility, and abundance
Carnelian	Red/orange	Wards off negative energies, inspires courage
Citrine	Yellow	Aids self-confidence, renewal, useful dreams
Hematite	Silver/grey/shiny black	Strengthens willpower and confidence, helps with problem solving
Lapis Lazuli	Blue/dark blue	Helps with altered consciousness, meditation, divination
Moonstone	White/pale blue	Used in Goddess rituals, good for intuition and wisdom
Quartz Crystal	White/clear	Promotes healing, clarity, spiritual development
Rose Quartz	Pink	Promotes emotional healing, love and friendship
Tiger's Eye	Brown/tan/gold with bands of black	Protection, energy

TABLE THREE:
HERBS AND ESSENTIAL OILS

Herb	General Magical Uses
Basil	Fosters loving vibrations, protection, wards off negativities in a home
Chamomile	Brings love, healing, relieves stressful situations
Rosemary	Love and lust spells, promotes healthy rest
Thyme	Attracts loyalty, affection, psychic abilities
Valerian	Protection, drives away negativity, purifies sacred space

Essential Oil	General Magical Uses
Bergamot	Promotes energy, success, prosperity
Cinnamon	Increases psychic connections, promotes healing, success, luck
Clove	Protection, courage, banishing negative energies, cleanses auras
Eucalyptus	Healing and purification
Jasmine	Strengthens intuition and inspiration, promotes sensuality and love
Lavender	Healing, cleansing, removing anxiety
Sandalwood	Clears negativity, promotes balanced energy flow

SUGGESTIONS FOR FURTHER READING

Please note that this is a very brief list. Many other interesting and useful resources are available in print and online.

History of Traditional Wicca

Gerald Gardner, *Witchcraft Today* (1955) and *The Meaning of Witchcraft* (1959)

Doreen Valiente, *Where Witchcraft Lives* (1962)

Raymond Buckland, *Witchcraft....The Religion* (1966)

Margot Adler, *Drawing Down the Moon: Witches, Druids, Goddess-Worshippers, and Other Pagans in America* (1979)

Sybil Leek, *The Complete Art of Witchcraft* (1971)

Contemporary Wicca and Witchcraft

Janet and Steward Farrar, *Eight Sabbats for Witches* (1981)

Scott Cunningham, *Wicca: A Guide for the Solitary Practitioner* (1989)

Ellen Dugan, *Natural Witchery: Intuitive, Personal & Practical Magick* (2007)

Laurie Cabot with Tom Cowan, *Power of the Witch: The Earth, the Moon, and the Magical Path to Enlightenment* (1990)

D.J. Conway, *Celtic Magic* (1990)

Science and Magic

Itzhak Bentov, *Stalking the Wild Pendulum: On the Mechanics of Consciousness* (1977)

John C. Briggs and F. David Peat, *Looking Glass Universe: The Emerging Science of Wholeness* (1986)

F. David Peat, *Synchronicity: The Bridge between Matter and Mind* (1987)

Fritjof Capra, *The Tao of Physics: An Exploration of the Parallels Between Modern Physics and Eastern Mysticism* (2010)

WICCA

FINDING
YOUR PATH

A Beginner's Guide to Wiccan Traditions,
Solitary Practitioners, Eclectic Witches,
Covens, and Circles

LISA CHAMBERLAIN

CONTENTS

INTRODUCTION

Despite the many social inroads made by Wiccans and other witches over the last few decades, confusion and stereotypes about this rich and unique religious belief system still persist in our mainstream culture.

Those who are brave enough to declare themselves witches are often still met with stares of disbelief, outright laughter, or concerned questioning about their mental state, even from well-meaning friends.

Yes, there are still plenty among us who think that witches are only fictional characters from fairy tales, movies, and books. And despite the better reputation that our more contemporary fictional witches (and "wizards") have been getting, many people still associate the "w" word with wicked intentions and evil deeds.

But those who take the time to explore Wicca with an open mind will always discover that Wiccan witches follow an ethical moral code, which can be summed up simply as "harm none."

And this is only one way in which actual witches—Wiccan or non-Wiccan—defy the old stereotypes. Wiccans are not malicious supernatural beings flying around on broomsticks and boiling reptiles in cauldrons. Wiccans are healers, soothsayers, wise-women and wise-men, spiritual counselors, herbalists, gardeners, astrologers, animal-lovers, and, just like every single being on Earth, inherently part of the divine.

Welcome to this introductory guide to the practice of Wicca, an earth-based religion of polytheistic pagan worship, reverence for nature, and magical witchcraft.

While Wicca is a modern religion, it is based on and inspired by pre-Christian pagan practices, often referred to by participants as "the Old Religion." It has many forms and traditions, most of which are also influenced by esoteric elements of the Western Mystery Tradition as it was developed in the Middle Ages, including the mystical philosophy of the Kabbalah, alchemy, the role of the Elements, and more. Some forms of Wicca also make use of older systems of astrology, and even divination practices like Tarot cards and runes.

Then, of course, there's magic (or "magick" as many prefer to spell it), which, for those who practice it, goes hand-in-hand with the concepts and tenets held within the Wiccan belief system.

Now would be a good time to point out that not all Wiccans practice magic, and not all consider themselves to be "witches."

However, since the original practitioners of what we now call Wicca did both, this guide considers Wiccans in general to be witches who practice magic, with all due respect to those who differ in these regards, and who are still considered to be included in this guide, which focuses on the wide variety of ways in which contemporary Wicca is practiced today.

Wicca began as a group-centered practice taking place within covens—a coven being, of course, a group or gathering of witches for the purpose of conducting ritual or magic.

These covens originally operated in secrecy—and many still do—in keeping with the idea that witches had been meeting in such a way, secretly, throughout the Christianization of Europe and the persecution of pagans that followed.

While it later turned out that this wasn't exactly the case, the new-found "tradition" of covens proved very beneficial to the growth of witchcraft in its revived form. Witches coming together in covens to study their Craft, create and adapt new practices, and spread their knowledge to others was indeed the vehicle for the rise of Wicca, first in Europe and then in the United States and beyond.

This guide will, of course, cover the basic institution of the coven, but will also introduce you to the wider spectrum of contemporary Wiccan practice, moving from the traditional, "orthodox" covens to looser, more "eclectic" covens and circles, and then on to the more recent phenomenon of solitary practice, which has appealed to both traditional and eclectic Wiccans alike.

You will also be introduced to a handful of the main Wiccan traditions practiced today, as well as the concept of eclectic Wicca, which has been the fastest growing form over the past few decades. If you don't already have a sense of the amazing diversity of this innovative religion, you certainly will by the end of this book!

Whether you're considering pursuing Wicca as a spiritual path, or would simply like to know more about it, this guide is a great place to start.

As a matter of fact, Wicca is one of the world's few religions that is as likely to be studied entirely on one's own through reading as through in-person guidance from other practitioners. Unlike a sect of Christianity or Judaism, for example, there aren't a lot of opportunities to sit in on a religious service to see what it's like.

Depending on where you live, you might be able to find a Wiccan circle or even an "open" coven where you can witness a sabbat celebration or other ritual, but if not, you're pretty much on your own.

Of course, the Internet provides plenty of resources and opportunities to discuss the Craft with others, and this has proved immensely valuable to new and experienced Wiccans alike. But do be aware that the open, "democratic" nature of the Internet has its drawbacks—chiefly that anyone can present any information they like, whether it's accurate or not.

The best way to make sure you're getting a solid education in Wicca is to read widely and voraciously, but it's equally important to pay attention to what your intuition is telling you as you absorb the information. The reason there are so many forms of Wicca is that there are countless ways to understand and experience its core essence, and it will likely take a while for you to discover where your individual path begins.

As you grow in your knowledge and experience of the Craft, you just may find that it has become more than an interest in a religion, but a rewarding way of life. May everything that you read within be of service to you on your journey, and let love and light guide you toward the path that is best for you. Blessed Be.

WITCHCRAFT:
A BRIEF OVERVIEW OF
HISTORY AND
SECRECY

The use of witchcraft goes back as far as the outer edges of our human record, and probably farther. It is possibly as old as civilization itself.

In 3100 B.C., ancient Egyptians worshiped under a polytheistic belief system, and we have evidence that this included sorcery. In the pre-Christian worlds of the Norse, Celts, Greeks, Romans, and Indians, working with herbs, stones, and magic words was very commonplace, as was a visit to a seer to ask questions about how a battle, invasion, or life in general was going to turn out.

Flashing forward to the era when Jesus was alive, we can see that the magical arts were still widely practiced, as there are several references to them in the Bible.

And the witch trials in both Europe and the New World of the 16th and 17th centuries show the belief in witchcraft still going strong in the late Middle Ages—though by this time, of course, the way in which those who practiced the craft were viewed was distorted by religious propaganda and paranoia.

Indeed, the misrepresentation of witchcraft seems to be its own "tradition," going back, in some places, nearly two thousand years.

The leaders of the Roman Catholic Church needed to eradicate all forms of paganism in order for their own religion to truly take hold, and so gradually witchcraft became associated with the Christian ideas of "evil" and "Satan."

Thus, people who saw fit to continue practicing were forced to retreat under the hood of night for fear of being punished, excommunicated, or even worse, executed. It was an ugly time that all but eradicated the old ways, and secrecy is the only thing that kept its remnants alive.

Many modern covens and solitary witches have preserved this tradition of secrecy, believing that quiet and privacy for practitioners is still of utmost importance, and with good reason. Magic and rituals aren't a novelty, and their impact is far-reaching.

Besides, there is also a lingering fear of persecution in the community, which is surprising yet still common for Wiccans to endure. Indeed, mainstream views of witchcraft in modern times are also, unfortunately, still a bit muddled due to the false images of witches we see in movies, books, and other forms of media.

Even in a world where you can summon a Wiccan Priestess for your last rites in hospital, there are sneers and jeers. Many practitioners feel it is simply better just to keep quiet and do as one will.

Unfortunately, the secrecy of centuries past, plus the near-eradication of the old religion, means that we don't have a lot of concrete information about how our ancestors practiced what we now call witchcraft. We don't even know for sure exactly when or how covens came into the picture. While the first historical references we find to covens in the Western world date back to the 16th century, we just don't know much beyond that.

Nonetheless, the coven today is a long-revered institution that guards the secrets of the craft while ensuring its survival, and this is thanks to the work of the spiritual pioneers of the late 19th and early 20th centuries.

THE BIRTH OF WICCA

The late 19th century saw the revival of a variety of occult arts in Britain, where many spiritual enthusiasts met, exchanged ideas, and formed groups and societies for the purpose of further pursuing their interests.

One such group was the Hermetic Order of The Golden Dawn, a kind of coven in its own right whose members studied and practiced magic as well as divination, contacting spirits, and all things esoteric.

The beginnings of modern Wicca really originated here, when the British occultist and author Aleister Crowley was taken under The Golden Dawn's wing in the early 1900s. Crowley's work and writings became highly influential for another occultist who came along a few decades later—Gerald Gardner.

Gerald Gardner is considered to be the "father of modern witchcraft." Others call him the "grandfather of Wicca." He was a British occult enthusiast and writer who trained under the Rosicrucian Order, where he met a few friends who ultimately introduced him to a group called the New Forest Coven, into which he was initiated.

From these coveners, whose identities remain mysterious today, Gardner learned rituals, magic, and other lore dating back to earlier times. He combined this with the inspiration he drew from the writings of Aleister Crowley to start his own coven, which he called Bricket Wood.

Over the next few years, he developed his framework for witchcraft which we now call Gardnerian Wicca. And although the full extent of the specific beliefs, rituals, and other practices involved in Traditional Gardnerian Wicca are known only to initiates of Gardnerian covens— in keeping with the tradition of secrecy—it is this framework that much of modern Wiccan practice is based on, whether it's coven-based, solitary, or even eclectic.

WICCA TRADITIONS

From Gardner's form of the craft (which he never called "Wicca," by the way—that came later), other traditions developed. Initiates in Gardner's lineage went on to form Alexandrian and Seax Wicca, just to name a couple.

The continuing development of this very diverse religion has gotten to the point where there are probably more Wiccan paths than can be described in one book—particularly if you include eclectic practitioners in the mix. However, those new to the Craft who are reading around on the Internet and in print are most likely to encounter one of three main "branches" on the tree of Wicca—Gardnerian, Alexandrian, or Dianic—either in their "pure form" or in forms loosely based on the original.

These three, along with a few other more commonly encountered traditions, will be discussed in further detail later in this guide.

What's the difference between one tradition and another?

Each Wiccan tradition has its own way of practicing the religion: the protocols for rituals, the deities to worship, the structure of worship, how a coven is organized, and any number of other details large and small may differ from one tradition to the next.

Two Wiccan traditions may have some of the same things in common, such as a similar way to begin a sabbat ritual, but differ widely in other ways, such as the pantheon their patron deities are selected from.

While there are set rules in each tradition, it's generally understood that covens and solitary practitioners alike may add to the tradition's teachings and adapt the rules as necessary, so long as the tradition's main teachings remain intact. This will depend on how "orthodox" the coven or solitary prefers to be.

Of course, once too many changes are made, the tradition is no longer being followed, which means it's likely that a new tradition is being formed.

Do I have to follow a specific tradition?

In essence, all Wiccans use the work and beliefs of one tradition or another, at least to some extent.

Unless you're literally making up every single aspect of your practice (in which case, you're not actually practicing Wicca), then you're following in the footsteps of those who came before you.

That being said, there's a lot of variety in terms of how strictly any given Wiccan adheres to the "way it's always been" along a particular path.

Covens typically follow specific Wiccan traditions that dictate their structure, rituals, and spell-work. While covens tend to adhere pretty strictly to their tradition, they may from time to time make exceptions, but this will depend on a unique set of circumstances that prevail in the group.

Solitary practitioners also follow traditions. Some follow a specific tradition as closely as they can, while other prefer to put their own twist on older versions of practice.

Some people follow many different aspects of several traditions, preferring to mix and match. This is called Eclectic Wicca, something that we'll look deeper at a little later.

Finding and following a tradition in Wicca is a wonderful thing because it's a way to learn and grow into your shoes, so to speak. It can be a great feeling to know that you found the right religion for you, and this is what following a tradition can provide.

Sometimes there can be some trial and error involved, though. If you're checking out a coven in your area and find that the tradition the coven is following isn't exactly what you had envisioned for yourself, simply search for other options and learn as much as you can along the way until you find the perfect fit.

That is, of course, one of the most appealing parts of being Wiccan: the ability to adapt and grow into the right path. You may even find yours by starting with an established tradition, and then moving on to your own eclectic practice. This approach is great for the independently-minded newbie.

Just keep in mind that wherever your ultimate path leads you, knowledge is crucial, so you should always be willing to learn—whether it be from books like this one, or from a coven or circle in your area. We'll take a closer look at these "in-person" options in the next few sections of this guide.

PART ONE

COVENS, CIRCLES, AND SOLITARY PRACTITIONERS

AN INTRODUCTION TO COVENS

Because covens seem to be the most complex of the many ways that Wiccans practice, this is a good time to look deeper into these rather secretive groups.

Yes, covens are still usually secretive, both in the spirit of tradition and as a way to protect the energy and activity in their circles from interference from the outside world.

So what exactly is a coven? What do its members do? How do covens work, and why do so many people gravitate towards them? Is it wise to join a coven, and if you do, what are the benefits and potential pitfalls of doing so?

These are all good questions. In this section, we'll be trying to answer them.

SPIRITUAL COMMUNITY AND TREASURE TROVE OF KNOWLEDGE

While the solitary and/or eclectic path has plenty of appeal, many people who are new to Wicca do seem inexplicably called to join a coven. So what is the pull?

Many feel that because the practice of gathering together for magical purposes was exercised back as far as ancient times, that this is the right way to observe such traditions. Others feel that joining a coven is an important part of becoming Wiccan and that the only way to become a Wiccan is through the most traditional of means possible. Furthermore, there are those who feel that they could benefit greatly from the knowledge and spiritual teachings of others and wish to congregate for the purpose of learning.

Each of these is a very valid reason for wishing to join and regularly attend the proceedings of a coven.

You might say that traditionalism and the conservation of old ways is held near and dear in terms of practicing most, if not all, religions.

Even the Roman Catholic Church has a hierarchical structure and a priesthood with an air of exclusivity. Convents are also much like covens, and some may even find it interesting that the two words have somewhat related etymologies. Buddhist monks gather for spiritual reasons and, like nuns, live together and dedicate their entire existence to learning the spiritual teachings of their chosen path. Then there are gurus and swamis, the ancient Druids, and a litany of many more spiritual societies.

Those practicing modern Paganism might consider the Druids to be a great example of a type of "coven before its time," given how much work was put into developing magical abilities, healing, and studying the mysteries hidden from plain view. Druids were not alone, however.

Shamans, herbalists, Native Americans, Ancient Egyptians, Greeks, and many more had fraternal orders that allowed for the working of magic as well as healing and worship of the divine.

Because we all want to be as close to our roots as possible, it makes perfect sense for Wiccans to seek to join covens in order to preserve a tradition that could very well be dying out due to the influx of solitary practitioners, eclectic Wiccans, and generalized circles popping up all over the place.

Covens do at times feel threatened by the impending extinction of their lines. Fortunately, there are plenty of newcomers to Wicca who are inclined to be purists when it comes to their religion. It's completely natural to want to fully immerse yourself in a new spiritual leaning. It's the only way for some, and this means seeking out a coven that is accepting new members and possibly even going through the same initiation rituals Gerald Gardner first introduced all those decades ago.

Purists, as we all know, are going to be driven in their purpose, learning as many of the old ways as possible because their general attitude is that joining a coven is the only right way to become Wiccan and sustain a 'true' Wiccan path. We know that this isn't true anymore, but if seeking out and joining a coven is what makes you feel the most at home in the faith, by all means do so. After all, there is no right or wrong way to follow this deeply spiritual and earth-attuned path.

Finally, we know that covens are treasure troves of information on the craft and its tenets. Their members join together and exchange knowledge, putting it all into practice, learning exponentially as the group gets older and wiser as a whole. Those looking to be formally initiated into covens may be enticed by the prospect of benefiting from this knowledge in their own solo work, in addition to their participation in the group.

While some see this as a selfish desire for personal gain, this is actually one of the reasons that covens bring in new members: to pass on the information and teachings they possess.

If the Hermetic Order of The Golden Dawn had never adopted Aleister Crowley into their circle, Gerald Gardner wouldn't have had so much magical inspiration and information to work with himself. The need to learn is within all of us, and that is never a selfish pursuit, so if this is your aim, you have arrived at the right place by looking into covens and what they do.

All of these are very good reasons to research covens and become a member of one. Without these motives, we wouldn't have these special spiritual societies in this day and age, and thus, this unique aspect of the faith would wither away into the past.

THE COVEN LIFE

Because of the tradition of secrecy in most covens, and because each coven is unique, it's a bit difficult to get into specific detail about what it's like to belong to one.

But by now, you at least know that a coven isn't just a bunch of cackling hags around a bubbling cauldron. A coven is a community of

Wiccans who are dedicated to the Craft and its teachings, as well as, usually, a specific tradition of it.

These special groups are sometimes quite old, with lineage dating back as far as the 1960s, but there are always new groups developing as well, who carry on the old traditions while perhaps adding some of their own.

Covens perform a lot of great rituals, sabbats, and healing circles. They also do handfastings, naming ceremonies, and much more. They can heal people, hold prayer circles, and use their knowledge to spread love and light in the world around them.

TRADITIONAL COVEN STRUCTURES

The coven is traditionally made up of anywhere from nine to thirteen members, but in modern times, some groups like to allow larger numbers in order to include family members. Others keep their group smaller—with as few as three members—for a more intimate circle.

There is usually a hierarchical structure to traditional covens. Generally, there are "degrees," or ranks, that initiates can make their way through by studying and learning from elders in the Craft.

There are typically three different degrees, with the First being the most basic requirement for initiation. The Second and Third Degrees permit more responsibility and activity within the coven leadership.

The coven leader, or leaders, will make larger decisions affecting the coven and will preside over important rituals.

Typically, a more traditional coven will have one or two leaders. If there is only one, it will be a female who is referred to as the High Priestess.

The High Priestess is considered to be the center of all rituals and magic. She makes the coven's bigger decisions and evaluates prospective members to ensure that they are ready to enter initiation. She also decides whether members who want to pursue initiation into a higher degree are ready to do so.

If there is a second leader, it will be a male who is referred to as the High Priest. Traditionally, the High Priest was subordinate to the High Priestess, and this is still true in some covens, but many, even those who descend from the original Gardnerian and Alexandrian traditions, have opted for a more equal sharing of power between their leaders.

The High Priest and Priestess are highly knowledgeable in the craft and may be elders in the group. They may have even have come up through the ranks of the coven themselves, if the coven has been around long enough, finally reaching the top level of leadership.

Just beneath the High Priest and Priestess are the members of the Inner Court.

The Inner Court is the group of witches who have completed at least the Second Degrees of initiation and have proven themselves wholly proficient in both their ritual and spell-work.

The Third Degree Practitioners are the ones who are most well-versed and are being positioned to start and manage a coven of their own, if they desire to do so. These witches are closest to the leaders and are often present in the sacred circle during specific rituals and magic undertakings. They also help to teach the people in the coven's Outer Circle who are seeking First Degree initiation.

Second Degree initiates are at a level where they are allowed to be a part of the circle and are deepening their knowledge of the coven's ritual work while helping with the non-initiates. They are taught by the Priestess and Third Degree members at an accelerated rate, illustrating the importance of their role in the coven. Some Second Degree witches will even have the ability to train First Degrees if they have proven themselves ready. This could also indicate a Second Degree witch who is ready for initiation into the Third Degree.

Speaking of this type of advancement, it's useful to note that one of the big taboos in many covens with hierarchies is when a Second Degree initiate asks to be moved up to the final level, rather than being invited.

This major faux pas may even see you removed from the coven if the Priestess is upset enough (although it would be hard to imagine, it does happen. Hierarchy can have interesting effects on the human ego).

The First Degree witches are those who have just been initiated into the craft. They are in a rank of their own, separate from both the Outer and Inner Circles.

First Degree practitioners have shown that they are pure in intention, that they have the desire and passion to learn, and have a basic understanding of magic and rituals. This level of initiation allows members to learn how to cast a circle in their particular coven, undergoing training from those in the higher ranks. Once they have proven themselves proficient and dedicated, they may be initiated into the Second Degree, but as with all levels, only with the Priestess's blessing.

The Outer Circle is occupied by those who would like to be initiated into the coven. They are not present for everything that the coven does, often being closed out of more important or sacred rituals and esbats. This is to protect the coven from those with ill intentions or those who are simply not ready to begin progressing on their path.

In the Outer Circle, one is still in the process of becoming educated and proving of one's self to the coven and its leader(s). They are not always even considered to be "members" until they are initiated into the First Degree, and they cannot enter the First Degree unless the higher ranks approve.

Looking at this rigid structure, one can see how serious and devout coven members must be to become a part of the main circle. It may seem rather elaborate, but this is the traditional structure that covens followed back in the early days of Wicca.

There are many groups that still observe this hierarchy today, although others have simplified things a bit. It all depends on the coven's tradition and the preferences of the coveners.

NEWER ADAPTATIONS

In terms of equality and views of power structures, the world has come a long way since the mid-1950s when the traditional coven structure was ingrained into modern witchcraft.

In the decades since, and particularly in the 21st century, many Wiccans have adapted the old rules to make them more practical and appropriate to their own experience of society.

For example, the traditional supremacy of the High Priestess was meant, in part, to balance out the gender inequalities of British society in the middle of the last century. While it can be argued that the world still has a long way to go toward achieving total equality, many contemporary Wiccans have come to see this aspect of the traditional coven structure as unnecessary and even cumbersome. Therefore, the High Priestess and High Priest may share power equally in many modern-day covens.

Another variation is the complete and total abolishing of degrees. This makes for fewer issues among the ranks because, well, there are none. It also prevents dissent that can arise from feeling pinned under such a limiting authority figure of sorts. Without degrees, people feel more at ease to practice and learn at their own pace instead of trying to cram three centuries' worth of information into their brains in order to make the next rank.

Moreover, some covens do not allow for an Outer Circle. The High Priestess may interview perspective members or the coven may advertise when it is open to new initiates, closing itself off from new memberships for a large majority of the time. This keeps all of the coven's proceedings from being seen by people who might decide not to join, but will still know about—and might even go around speaking of—details relating to of the coven's work.

Another system that people find preferable over the traditional coven structure is an electoral system, whereby the High Priest and Priestess are voted on by the members of the coven.

This can be tricky, depending on the maturity level of all the egos involved, because influence may have nothing to do with who is most deserving or learned. However, when members are being responsible and letting divine forces inform their decisions, the results can be very satisfying.

As you can see, there are several different possibilities for how a given coven is structured and operated.

The extent to which hierarchy is observed is one of the things you'll want to inquire about when looking into joining a coven. You'll also want to know about the general rules and requirements.

It tends to go without saying that coven members are expected to attend every meeting and every ritual (at least, those which they are permitted to attend, depending on their rank). They may also be restricted to practicing magic within the coven's circle alone, prohibited from doing their own solo work until initiated into a higher level (or, in some covens, not at all). Each group will conduct all of its rituals in a specific way that is traditional to their circle, and some will only allow one copy of the coven's Book of Shadows to exist.

Of course some covens are much more rule-oriented than others, but because all are closed to the public, there is no way of knowing just how strict a given coven may be until you approach them with your interest in joining. Before you start knocking on doors, however, it's useful to take a closer look at the benefits and potential drawbacks of choosing this path of Wiccan practice.

THE PROS AND CONS OF COVENS

As with any decision involving spirituality, the choice of whether or not to join a coven should not be taken lightly.

Coven membership is a serious commitment, and it requires careful consideration. You will have to be honest with yourself about whether you are willing to go the distance.

Even if it sounds like a very exciting idea at first, it is important to evaluate each potential advantage and each possible drawback before you can be certain whether coven life is for you.

THE BENEFITS OF JOINING A COVEN

Becoming a member of a coven can bring many blessings that may end up being very important to your spiritual path.

Perhaps the main benefit of joining a coven is the obvious acceleration in learning. You will be training yourself in Wicca actively, learning each and every skill the coven views as essential.

In addition, a number of knowledgeable members with unique perspectives on the Craft will be taking you under their wing, which means you have the potential to learn a very diverse skill set.

Many coven members like the sense of community that a coven can provide. It gives them a feeling of belonging in a world that isn't entirely open to the tenets of Wicca. As just about anyone in the faith can tell you, it can feel a tad lonely to be the only Wiccan in a room of Christians and Atheists.

Being a part of a coven gives Wiccan practitioners something to belong to and somewhere to practice their religion with others who share a common spiritual orientation. This sense of community is really no different from what Christians, Muslims, and Jews enjoy in their own congregations.

Some hold the view that the magic worked as part of a coven is much more powerful than that of a solitary practitioner. This is why people so often form circles (groups that are their own entity separate from covens) for doing rituals and spell-work.

This may or may not be true, depending on how intent and focused the group is and whether the work is really done correctly. If you consider the potential power of the raising of energy in covens, it could be really quite spectacular, but that doesn't necessarily mean that the energy raised by a solitary witch is any less authentic.

Others like to be led by someone with a vast amount of wisdom, and find that being a part of a coven allows them to do so freely without having to do the heavy thinking for the group. There is also a lesson in commitment here that people enjoy learning. This is something that covens teach through mandatory attendance, a vow of secrecy, and a hierarchical structure to make one's way up through.

THE DRAWBACKS OF WORKING IN A COVEN

Those who have tried covens and found it not to be their best option have tended to feel a lack of spiritual freedom. Some would even go far enough to call it dogma.

Being a part of a coven can mean following a very rigid system where everything must be done a certain way. Its members can also be less than forgiving of those who break any of the rules, as they are seen to be going against the coven and betraying trust.

So you may have to weigh "the good of the group" against your own personal preferences at times, and not all aspiring Wiccans are quite cut out for this way of being.

Some covens don't actually allow many, or any, of their members to progress beyond a specific degree, preventing them from being able to leave the group and start their own coven or even having an intimate part in rituals and spell-work. In fact, certain covens don't allow for spell-casting outside of their circle, figuratively and spiritually cutting members off at the knees and keeping them at arm's length from the Goddess and God.

This is much like what cults and even some churches do to their followers and should be a red flag for anyone wishing to truly progress along their spiritual path.

Because attendance is generally mandatory for anyone who is initiated into a coven, it can be difficult to wedge coven participation into one's lifestyle. Not everyone can commit to something that requires them to come out for every esbat, sabbat, and spell-casting there is in a year, so it is best to consider this in terms of practicality.

Can you attend every meeting a coven holds in addition to taking care of all of your other commitments?

If not, you may need to reduce your other activities to create a less hectic life—which isn't a bad idea for anyone, really—or else stick to the solitary path. (Another option is to join a circle, rather than a coven, as circles usually have less demanding requirements. Circles will be discussed in the next section, below.)

Finally, some find it difficult to feel an intimate level of connection with their spell and ritual work if they are a part of a group, as they don't feel to be "in the driver's seat" of their own spiritual path.

This is another potential reason to try a circle first, to see if you can work with others and still feel as connected and focused on the earth and your task.

SOME GENTLE
WORDS OF CAUTION

Even though we live in a world where religion should be a safe thing to come together for, there are some unscrupulous people out there who will engage in unethical and even dangerous activities in the name of Wicca.

Unfortunately, you do have to take some important precautions when it comes to looking into covens. If you are becoming a part of one and notice any of the following behaviors on the part of your would-be fellow coveners, you are strongly advised to leave the group immediately. Depending on the circumstances, you may even want to report certain activities to the police.

Cult-like Atmosphere or Proceedings

If you find that the coven you have joined seems more interested in worshiping its leaders rather than the God and Goddess, it might be time to go before you're trapped in something you cannot get out of.

Cult leaders always start out appearing to be about a religion or spiritual path, but end up being about absolute control over their followers. Cults can be dangerous when people are brainwashed into doing risky and/or illegal things or giving up everything they have to a leader.

Satanic and Malevolent Work

Wicca is a religion of Threefold Law, and there should never be a situation where a coven is doing a spell that will harm anyone or anything.

The same goes for anything resembling "devil-worship" (Wiccans do not classically believe in "Satan") and/or making "sacrifices."

If you witness anything like this, turn around and walk in the other direction.

Covens that participate in these kinds of works are not Wiccan and can really destroy your life with their dark magic and poor reputations.

While there are NeoPagan groups who worship a deity named Satan in a pre-Biblical sense, Satanism is not Wicca and should not be confused with the Goddess-and-God-worshiping path.

Illegal Activities and Drug-Taking

If you find yourself in the middle of a "coven" gathering where there is illegal activity happening, this is a good time to remove yourself from their company.

Theft and vandalism are not a part of Wicca and go against its tenets, but unfortunately there are occasional miscreants who try to use the secrecy of coven work as a smokescreen to hide their juvenile antics. As for drug use, it isn't ever a good idea to take something that someone gives to you unless you know exactly what's in it and what it's for.

Although some Pagan and NeoPagan groups use entheogenic drugs to attain heightened states of consciousness, taking drugs is dangerous, not to mention illegal, and you never know what you could be in for once they kick in.

Sexual Assault

Although many covens no longer operate in the nude or re-enact the union of the God and Goddess physically, some do, and so they often attract people with the wrong motives.

It's also possible that the use of ritual nudity and/or ritual sex is kept secret from new members, who will find the coven very appealing until it starts to get weird. Never become or remain a part of a coven where this kind of stuff is taking place (unless you're entirely comfortable with it), and if you witness anything physical happening against anyone's will, report it to the police.

Note: *These warnings may seem stern, but unfortunately they've been proven necessary through experience. They are not intended to scare you out of looking into initiation through a coven, however. Certainly, not every coven out there is a cult or a dangerous place to lure women and minors to—the incidents described above represent a very small minority. Nonetheless, it's always better to be safe than sorry, so keep your sixth sense primed for anything that seems off about a group you come into contact with.*

THE WICCAN CIRCLE: AN ALTERNATIVE TO THE COVEN

You may or may not have heard of "circles" before in your explorations of Wicca.

A circle is much like a coven in that it is a group of people coming together for the purpose of ritual worship and spellwork. It is also a big place of learning, both for newcomers to the Craft and for solitaries who are looking to find a sense of community in their practice.

This relatively new form of spiritual community has evolved out of a desire for less structure and less hierarchy than what is typically experienced in a traditional coven.

While you may see both circles and covens advertised in the same sections of online forums and directories, there are significant differences between these two types of Wiccan groups.

For starters, covens are generally exclusive, and often are not open to new members. You typically can't just arrange to come in and be a part of a coven. A circle is much more open, with fluctuating membership, usually allowing new people to come and go in order to see if it is something they enjoy. In addition, circles tend not to follow a specific tradition. Some do, and they may ask that only those who practice under their tradition, or else are willing to learn, join them, but usually they're fairly eclectic groups that come together from many different traditions and backgrounds.

As indicated above, circles are much more informal than traditional covens. Circles come together to practice the Craft, but without developing any hierarchy among members. No initiation is required, and there are no degrees to move through. There are no High Priestesses or High Priests. Attendance at meetings and rituals is not mandatory. A circle is more like a club, which makes many people feel more at ease and in control of their own spiritual paths.

Of course, for some Wiccans, a "club" is a little *too* loose in terms of the bonds that can be formed through the long-term commitment involved in a coven. Having consistent membership creates a more solid group dynamic than might be possible in a circle. Nonetheless, circles can be an ideal way for solitary and eclectic witches to come together and discuss their religion with like-minded others, to have access to community for ritual and spellwork, and to keep learning as they pursue their path.

SOLITARY PRACTICE

As the name would imply, solitary practitioners are Wiccans who choose to practice the Craft on their own—in their homes, backyards, or out in nature.

While some coven members may do spellwork on their own, if their coven permits it, this is not the same thing as solitary practice. Though they may occasionally join a circle for a particular sabbat celebration or other special occasion, the vast majority of a solitary Wiccan's spiritual work is done alone, and there are plenty who never commune with others at all.

It's estimated that more than half of all Wiccans are solitary practitioners.

This trend came about toward the end of the 20th century, when interest in Wicca had become widespread thanks to many published books on the Craft. For many would-be practitioners, there wasn't a coven within 500 miles, or if there was, it either wasn't open to new membership, or just wasn't a good fit in terms of personalities.

So people began practicing on their own, leaving behind the notion that one could only become a Wiccan through initiation by another Wiccan. Instead, they began to self-initiate, and adapt other coven practices for solitary use.

REASONS FOR
CHOOSING A SOLITARY PATH

With the explosion of interest in Wicca in the age of the Internet, there are now many, many more covens out there in the world than there were just a few decades ago.

Nonetheless, there still isn't one in every single community, and again, even if there is one in your area, it may not be open to new members. Even if it is open, it may not be in the tradition you follow, or it may just not be a group you feel right about joining.

But lack of access to the coven of one's choice aside, there are several reasons why so many Wiccans choose a solitary path over a group pursuit.

For some, it really comes down to practicality. Frankly, it's much easier and more convenient to practice at home.

Gardnerian followers appreciate the freedom and comfort of working sky-clad for rituals, by themselves in their circle, with no prying eyes or inhibitions clouding their work. This also goes for witches who might be self-conscious in their ritual robes if others were to see them. In fact, for many solitaries, there's a lot to be said for the privacy of practicing behind closed doors.

It also works for those who have tight schedules and can't commit to the mandatory attendance expected of coven members—especially those with children.

You may remember that covens gather for spellwork, sabbats, and full moons, and sometimes new moons and special ceremonies. Not everyone can accommodate all of those occasions in addition to attending to the mundane events of life. Solitary practice allows for a 'when time allows' approach, and in this fast-paced world, this is a strong selling point for Wiccans who are up to their ears in life.

There's also the fact that solitaries can keep their faith entirely secret from the rest of the world, if they wish. Some Wiccans still have a lot of trepidation about identifying publicly with their religion, for fear of embarrassment, stigma, or other kinds of repercussions. While covens do practice secrecy, there's still no absolute guarantee that one would never be "outed" as a witch.

For other solitaries, the main attraction is freedom—to explore different traditions, to identify their own beliefs, to practice the kind of magic they want, and to basically just do their own thing.

In covens, rituals are usually set in stone, performed exactly according to the tradition's ways (with perhaps a few minor tweaks). In the solitary experience, rituals and spell-work can be much more fluid, with individual changes that would not be permitted in the more orthodox Wiccan traditions. On your own, you can decide for yourself how and where you cast a circle and the tools you use within it, and no one is there to tell you you're doing it incorrectly.

This also goes for pantheons and deities. There are a great many practitioners out there who crave the freedom to work the pantheon and/or deities they find to be most inspiring and evocative. When work within a coven, you are generally expected to follow their set of deities and their concept of the divine.

If you're fortunate enough to belong to a coven or circle that does share the same beliefs and ideas, that's wonderful, but this isn't always the case, and you can't force yourself to believe in something that doesn't feel right. Sometimes breaking away from the group is the only way to achieve your personal spiritual goals.

Finally, some believe that their energy is much more focused in their work when they do it alone.

It might be simply too distracting for practitioners to work with a group—there's a lot of activity going on when a coven performs a ritual or ceremonial magic. Others feel that their personal interests are not addressed by the group, or that the spellwork isn't personal because it is a collective effort towards one goal that they don't feel has anything to do with their lives. Service to others and to the greater world is good, but doing magic to effect change in one's own life is important too. Some solitary witches would simply prefer to work alone and focus their energy with laser-like precision on more personal pursuits or causes dear to their own hearts.

Solitary practice doesn't have to be a life-long commitment, though. You can always progress from working alone to joining your energies with like-minded others.

However, it can be a great place to start. If you are just beginning, you may find yourself unsure about which (if any) specific tradition you'd like to follow. The solitary approach means that you have the teachings and philosophies of several traditions at your fingertips. In fact, many coven members recommend spending time researching and studying on your own before deciding to join with others in your practice, so you start off with a clearer sense of what's right for you.

All in all, solitary practice has fewer rules in general. You can make and keep your own Book of Shadows, practice where and when you please, perform rituals to your liking, cast spells in the manner you feel most powerful, and worship the deities that you feel most at home with. You may not have the fellowship of others, but you are the leader of your own path.

Indeed, without the constraints of following a coven's rules and practices, the journey becomes a tailor-made experience.

SOME CONSIDERATIONS FOR THE SOLITARY PRACTITIONER

As you've no doubt concluded by now, solitary practice really is a completely different life from that of coven membership.

Being on one's own means grappling with and addressing certain aspects of the path in a different way. Here are some of the main elements of solitary practice that can present a challenge, at least at the beginning of the path.

Ethical Clarity

Although there's much more flexibility involved in practicing as a solitary versus as a coven member, this doesn't mean that it's a big free-for-all in terms of how one goes about the business of working magic.

Solitary practitioners are just as subject to the main Laws of Wicca as any member of a coven—namely, the Threefold Law and that very important line from the Wiccan Rede, "an it harm none."

"An it harm none, do what ye will" is generally considered to be the first rule of Wicca, and has often been presented as the only true rule. It means that as long as your actions do no harm to anyone—whether we're talking about spellwork or just how you go about your everyday life—then you should do what you want to do.

It's against Wiccan principles to work negative magic, of course, but it's also no good to work any kind of manipulative magic—in other words, anything that would interfere with another person's free will. If you think about it, you wouldn't want someone else doing anything to control your life or your actions, so it only makes sense that you shouldn't, either.

And for Wiccans who may be tempted to break, or even bend, this rule, the Threefold Law is there to make them think twice.

The Threefold Law, simply put, states that anything that you think, say, and do is sent out into the universe and then comes back at you three times as positively or negatively as the original thought, word, or action.

It can be likened to a ripple effect on a pond when a drop of rain hits it. At first, the circular ripples are very small, but they grow and spread out to become hundreds of times bigger than the very first ring. And when they reach the shore, they "bounce" off it and make their return journey back toward the center.

The same is true of how magical intentions operate on the spiritual plane. Understanding the Threefold Law is crucial to working successful magic without bringing negative consequences into your life.

Keeping this ripple metaphor in mind, there's also the need to remember that spellwork affects the entire Universe—not just the spellcaster or its intended recipient (if there is one).

It may not seem like the spellwork of one person could affect people down the street, in the next community, or across the world, but in actuality, one small incantation or knot tied at your altar could potentially have effects on those around you. This is why so many

Wiccans use the phrase "harm to none" when sealing their magical work.

One potential challenge then, for solitary practitioners, is the ability to think through their spellwork through before setting anything in motion that they cannot take back.

It's important to be very clear about one's motives and expectations in magical work. This can be difficult when you're wrapped up in emotions, or stressed out by a situation, and can't discern whether or how to try to solve a problem through magic.

Having no one to talk to about it can make the issue all that more challenging.

This doesn't mean that coven work is automatically fail-safe in the ethics department—Wiccans can go awry in groups just as easily as on their own—but that the perspectives and experiences of others can help refine one's magical choices.

Following Tradition

While many Wiccans choose the solitary path in order to create their own entirely unique practice, there are plenty others who still wish to follow a specific tradition, whether it be Gardnerian, Alexandrian, or even an offshoot of one of these.

Although most existing traditions were by and large built around covens—particularly Gardnerian and Alexandrian Wicca—they can, and have been, adapted for solitary practice. The challenges in doing so are that it can be harder to learn on one's own, even with the best of books, and there are aspects of ritual that don't translate from a group setting to a circle of one.

Furthermore, there's bound to be aspects of the practice that just can't be known about unless you're a coven initiate. So solitaries may find themselves having to adapt their individual practice in order to find what works best for them.

Adaptation should not be confused with "cheating" or doing something incorrectly, however.

First, it's important to remember that even Gardner adapted his coven's ritual liturgy over time, and Alex Sanders actually made adaptability part of his tradition's philosophy.

In many ways, it could be argued that adaptation is part of the tradition of Wicca as a whole. As long as you're following your chosen tradition as faithfully as you can, there's no reason to feel that you're not a true "Gardnerian" or "Alexandrian."

Sure, you're a solitary practitioner rather than a coven member, but why should that matter?

Avoiding the Endless "Label" Debates

Actually, to be frank, there are plenty of "orthodox" coven members who will tell you that it does matter, but they're speaking from their own perspective.

Many coveners still believe that it takes an initiated witch to make another witch, at least in their particular tradition. Yet solitary practitioners following these traditions will usually undertake a self-initiation, which they often describe as one of the most sacred and special experiences in their lifetime.

The fact is, no one has the authority to decree that one person is a Wiccan—Gardnerian or otherwise—and another is not.

It's true that self-initiation is seen as a sort of minimum requirement that one would want to have completed before calling oneself a Wiccan—just as you most likely wouldn't call yourself a Catholic unless you'd been converted and baptized into the faith.

Nonetheless, there's no one handing out "Wiccan certificates" to make your solitary practice official.

Covens can deny you initiation into their group, and it's their right to do so. But if you're choosing the solitary path, then you probably wouldn't have wanted to join them anyhow. (And even if the choice is only based on a lack of covens in your area, you might consider the possibility that you're actually meant for the solitary path.)

In the grand scheme of things, when it comes to "covens versus solitaries" or any other perceived point of debate among the huge diversity of Wiccans out there, mutual respect remains the ideal.

Don't get embroiled in arguments on the Internet (or in person) if you don't want to get bogged down in negative energy. No matter what path you choose in the Wiccan world, you know who you are, and no one else can tell you differently unless you let them.

MOVING FORWARD

Now that we've covered the differences between the coven life and the solitary path, and the benefits of each, it's time to take a look at some of the traditions you might choose from as you continue your explorations.

In the next sections, we'll briefly review some of the major traditions under the Wiccan umbrella. As always, pay attention to the signals your sixth sense sends to you as you read—it may be that a specific tradition jumps out at you right away, asking you to explore it further.

If this doesn't happen, no worries! It's still useful to have some background knowledge of available options as you seek your path.

PART TWO

WICCAN TRADITIONS

THE MOST POPULAR WICCAN TRADITIONS

You may already know that the term "Wicca" was never used by Gerald Gardner himself. Gardner referred to himself and his Bricket Wood coven members as "the Wica," but had no name beyond "witchcraft" in reference to their activities. "Wicca" didn't actually become a widely-recognized term until several years later.

Furthermore, Gardner never used the term "Gardnerian"—this was actually coined by another witch, Robert Cochrane, who ran in some of the same circles as Gardner back in the mid-20th century. Cochrane practiced his own form of the Craft and used "Gardnerian" as a way of distinguishing his own work from Gardner's.

This is all to say that what we think of as established terminology can have almost accidental origins. It's also a glimpse into how traditions are often born—by the splitting off of one or more practitioners from an established tradition into a new way of doing things.

Even within established traditions, such as Gardnerianism, there can be different branches practicing in slightly different ways, and as discussed above, every coven will have its own unique approach to the work. But there are still pretty clear boundaries between one tradition of Wicca and another.

Below, we'll take a look at three major limbs of the "tree" of Wicca—the Gardnerian, Alexandrian, and Dianic traditions—as these are the three you're most likely to encounter at the beginning of your exploration of this diverse religion.

THE GARDNERIAN TRADITION

Obviously, the Gardnerian Tradition is the oldest form of what we now call Wicca, having been developed in the 1950s, though some might argue that it originated with the witches Gerald Gardner trained under prior to creating his first magic compendium (High Magic's Aid) and creating the Bricket Wood Coven.

Gardner certainly attributed much of what he taught in his coven to a handful of witches belonging to what was called the New Forest Coven in the UK, but this isn't widely documented so it's hard to assert with confidence.

We do know that Gardner drew some of his information and inspiration from Aleister Crowley's works and the teachings of the Hermetic Order of the Golden Dawn, so there is consensus that the Gardnerian Tradition follows something older than the 20th century, in a combined form newly presented by Gardner.

Gardnerian Wiccans traditionally work in covens of 13 members, although this number can vary depending on the circumstances of the group. It's an initiatory tradition, meaning that one can only be initiated through another Gardnerian witch, so that every "true" Gardnerian can trace his or her lineage back to Gardner's original coven.

Gardner was an enthusiastic practitioner of nudism, which is where this element of the tradition came from, and the more orthodox Gardnerian covens today still practice ritual nudity.

The coven is led by a High Priestess, with a High Priest as "second in command," and this gender polarity is particularly important, as it reflects the mythical story of the sabbats, with the God being the deity who dies and is reborn year after year, while the Goddess is eternally alive.

The Gardnerian deities are the Horned God and the Mother Goddess, and they have specific names that are supposed to be kept secret from non-initiates. There is a great deal of emphasis on using the original Book of Shadows that Gardner created for rituals and magic, which is also supposed to be kept secret, although it has been published in a few different forms over the decades. Gardnerian rituals are highly elaborate in comparison to rituals in other traditions, and traditionally involved ritual sex, although this may or may not happen in present-day covens.

The three degrees of initiation discussed above in the coven section originated here, though they are probably borrowed from the traditions of older secret societies like the Freemasons and The Golden Dawn. Gardnerian covens are among the most secretive, making this tradition, at least in coven form, difficult to navigate for newcomers and curious outsiders.

THE ALEXANDRIAN TRADITION

Founded during the 1960s as an addendum to Gardnerian Wicca, the Alexandrian Tradition differs slightly from the original tradition in some interesting ways.

It was created by Alex Sanders and his wife Maxine, who were members of the Gardnerian Tradition and initiated into one of its covens in the early 60s.

The tradition was named "Alexandrian" by a friend and fellow witch, Stewart Farrar, in part because of Sanders' first name, but also in veneration of the Library of Alexandria. Constructed in the 3rd Century in Alexandria, Egypt, it was one of the first libraries in the world and housed a wealth of occult knowledge.

The Alexandrian Tradition is extensively covered in books by Stewart and Janet Farrar, authors and Wiccan practitioners who were both initiated into the main coven of the tradition by Maxine Sanders herself back in the 70s.

Alexandrian Wicca is similar to Gardnerian Wicca in many ways.

The High Priestess is the head of the coven, and there is a belief in the Goddess as well as a God. They also observe the three degrees of membership in a coven, although it differs slightly.

In terms of the worship of deities, however, there's an interesting twist: the Alexandrian Tradition follows the tale of the Holly King and his counterpart, the Oak King. Like the Gardnerian version, this tale is an ever-revolving wheel that coincides with the wheel of the year and explains the nature of each Wiccan sabbat perfectly:

The Oak King is born and conquers the dying Holly King. The Oak King then meets up with the maiden aspect of the Goddess in the early part of the year. They marry, and then the Goddess is impregnated. The Oak King comes to the height of his power during the Midsummer celebration, and the Goddess is ready to come into her mother form. As the Oak King's power begins to wane, we see the birth of the Holly King, who eventually slays the Oak King as the Goddess comes into her crone aspect during Midwinter.

Other differences between Gardnerian Wicca and Alexandrian Wicca include the choice to practice in clothing or ritual wear, and the presence of ceremonial magic and Hermeticism.

The tradition isn't necessarily quite as secretive or dogmatic. While there is some emphasis on the need to "follow the book" and its main teachings, there is a greater emphasis on growth and living out your own path, allowing for many changes and adjustments as practitioners see fit.

THE DIANIC TRADITION

Dianic Wicca takes a rather big departure from the older Wiccan traditions, and may be the first to come out of the United States rather than the UK.

The original and most well-known form of the tradition was founded in the 1970s by a woman named Zsuzsanna Budapest.

This is an all-female tradition, with a cosmology that focuses solely on the supremacy of the Goddess. As such, those who learn and study Dianic Wicca will mostly be monotheistic in a matriarchal system. There is an emphasis in this tradition on being politically and socially aware of the oppression and injustices faced by women.

This tradition typically does not have a hierarchical structure and is much freer in terms of spiritual growth and movement within the coven.

As in other traditions, Dianic Wiccans will meet on esbats, sabbats, and other significant times such as when a member or someone in the community is in need, but the work within these circles is very fluid and follows a woman-based approach in all things. There is a great deal of focus on emotional support here, and it isn't uncommon to find that women have entered Dianic covens or circles in order to heal themselves from some trauma or personal issue surrounding their femininity.

Another form of Wicca sharing the name "Dianic" was later started by Morgan McFarland and her husband, Mark Roberts, and this tradition does admit men, as do other traditions inspired by the original Dianic Wicca. However, those initiated through Budapest remain female-only.

A word of caution about the Dianic Traditions is that some practitioners will condone malevolent magic against those who harm women or cause them injustice through hexes, curses, and bindings. This is not a majority, however—most modern-day Dianic Wiccans will follow The Rede and Threefold Law.

OTHER TRADITIONS WITHIN THE WICCAN WORLD

The Gardnerian, Alexandrian, and Dianic Traditions may be the most widely practiced established traditions today, but there are many others, all with varying degrees of similarity to the older traditions.

One quite prominent tradition is Seax-Wica, a direct descendant of Gardnerian Wicca with an arguably more "American" feel, whose founder is often credited with bringing Wicca to the United States.

In more recent decades, several "cultural" forms have emerged that draw exclusively from a specific pantheon, rather than borrowing a Goddess from one pantheon and a God from another, which is fairly common in covens following the older traditions.

These "ethnic" traditions aim to translate the more "standard" Wiccan beliefs and practices into more culturally relevant forms in various ways.

We'll introduce two of these below, along with a final NeoPagan tradition that can be found across several forms of Wicca, and so deserves a mention here.

This is by no means an exhaustive list of Wiccan traditions, of course, but a brief overview of some of the more common forms that have taken root since the latter part of the twentieth century.

SEAX-WICA

Seax-Wica was also founded in the U.S. in the 1970s, by a British-born witch named Raymond Buckland.

Buckland had been a High Priest in the Gardnerian Tradition—the first in the U.S.—and started the first Gardnerian coven after moving to New York in the early 1960s.

After a decade of leading his Long Island Coven, however, he was growing more and more disenchanted with the way the hierarchical structure of Gardnerianism created politics and ego-battles in American initiates. He founded Seax-Wica as a way of continuing what was useful about Gardnerianism but in a fashion that was more suited to the culture of his new home.

Seax-Wica is inspired by Anglo-Saxon witchcraft as it was practiced in Anglo-Saxon England between the 5th and 11th centuries.

Its main deities are Woden and Freya, who represent the God and Goddess as found in the original Gardnerian Tradition. All the sabbats and esbats are celebrated. There is an emphasis on studying herbal lore and several forms of divination, including the Tarot and the Runes.

There are many differences between Seax-Wica and the more orthodox forms of Wicca.

For starters, there is no oath of secrecy, so it's not such a challenge to find out what goes on in covens, how they approach their rituals, etc. In fact, Buckland wrote a book, originally called The Tree and now republished as Buckland's Book of Saxon Witchcraft that serves as a guide to the tradition for any who would like to explore it. (It should be noted that this particular book assumes the reader already has a working knowledge of Wicca. If you don't, then be sure to check out Buckland's The Complete Book of Witchcraft to help you fill in the gaps.)

Furthermore, rituals and sabbat celebrations can be open, if the coven so chooses.

There is no Book of Shadows in this tradition, and adding new material to rituals, magic, etc. is welcomed if practitioners see fit.

There are no degrees of advancement as there are in other traditions, and coven leaders are democratically elected, serving a term of one lunar year (13 full moons). There is also no emphasis on lineage—in other words, being initiated by another Seax-Wica witch is not necessary. Self-dedication is recognized as a perfectly acceptable entry point to this form of the Craft.

NORSE WICCA

Just as Seax-Wica takes its inspiration from Anglo-Saxon pagan practices, Norse Wicca is infused with the beliefs, practices, and deities of the ancient Norse traditions of Scandinavia.

There is even a potential for some overlap between these two forms, since the pre-Christian Anglo-Saxon culture shares Germanic roots with the Norse culture of Scandinavia, and many similarities have been between the religions of the two areas—though it should be noted that more is known about the old Norse religion than about its Anglo-Saxon counterpart. And although Christianity did its best to eradicate these traditions, just as it did throughout pagan Europe, remnants of this rich culture are still with us today, in the form of Easter eggs, Christmas trees, and even five of our seven days of the week, named for Norse deities.

Unlike Seax-Wica, Norse Wicca is not an "official" tradition with a single founder, but rather an emerging trend among Wiccans who wish to work with a specific pantheon of deities and may draw inspiration from the ancient Norse sagas such as the Eddas and the Grimnismal. It's also common to adopt Germanic and Norse versions of sabbats, such as celebrating the Horse Fest at the Autumnal Equinox (often known as Mabon in traditional Wicca).

Working with runes is one element that many Norse Wiccans have in common with those in the Seax tradition. Runes originated in this culture as far back as 150 AD, and are thought to have served as both letters of an alphabet and magical talismans. Divination with runes is common among many NeoPagan paths, including other forms of Wicca.

One chief difference between what we might call "standard" or traditional Wicca and the Norse-influenced form is the potential for a richer and more nuanced sense of the afterlife. Indeed, the Norse religious belief system has a dense complexity that can make Wicca's beliefs and tenets seem rather two-dimensional in comparison. However, many followers of Norse Wicca adopt a syncretic approach, weaving the elements of the Norse system that resonate with them into their personal practice. Norse Wiccans tend to be solitary practitioners, with known covens being rather few and far between.

Norse Wicca should not be confused with Pagan reconstructionist religions such as Asatru or Odinism, whose followers aim to practice Norse religion as it truly existed in pre-Christian times. These reconstructionists, or "recons" for short, work only from verifiable historical sources, and actively distinguish their practice from that of Wiccans.

CELTIC WICCA/DRUIDIC WICCA

Also based in the belief system of an ancient world, Celtic Wicca and Druidic Wicca are technically two different traditions, though many Wiccans incorporate elements of both in their practice.

The Druids were the priestly class of Celtic society, serving as healers, poets, and philosophers, who practiced divination and magic as part of their role. Therefore, they were part of the fabric of Celtic life, and separating them out in order to practice strictly "Celtic Wicca" is definitely missing an important part of the picture.

Celtic Wiccans obviously work with deities of the Celtic pantheon—whether Irish, Welsh, Cornish, or even Gaulish (like the Germanic cultures, the Celts occupied a wide territory), and use Celtic names for sabbats, such as Lughnassa instead of Lammas.

The Ogham—a Celtic runic system—may be used in magical symbolism and divination, and some practitioners adopt the Celtic classification of elements rather than the standard Wiccan system.

Celtic covens may or may not involve a hierarchy or degrees of advancement—it depends on how much of Gardnerian or Alexandrian Traditions they wish to incorporate into their syncretic form of the Craft.

As for Druidic Wiccans, there is generally a focus on viewing all of nature as inherently divine, and all things as connected.

There is more of a metaphysical and shamanistic bent than what is found in more traditional Wicca. Animals are important to this belief system, particularly the stag, the salmon, the raven, the boar, and several others indigenous to ancient Ireland. An emphasis on herbal magic and sacred stones is also often part of this tradition.

Again, hierarchy may or may not be present in Druidic covens, but there is a greater likelihood of a more egalitarian structure than that found in more traditional Wicca.

Almost nothing is known about the specific magical and/or religious activities of the Druids, since they deliberately kept their knowledge in an oral tradition, so much of what is practiced today is inspired from Celtic mythology and the roles Druids play in these stories.

Most of what we know from written sources comes from a Christianized lens through monks recording the lore in medieval Ireland, and a solid amount from Celtic Wales has also survived, so Celtic and Druidic Wicca tend to have distinctly Irish and Welsh influences.

There are counterparts to the Norse Asatru and Odinism groups in this part of the world in the form of modern day "NeoDruids," as well as Celtic Reconstructionists. Both groups also distinguish themselves from Wicca, which is, of course, a religion of entirely modern origin, as opposed to a pre-Christian way of life being "reconstructed" in contemporary times.

FAERY WICCA

Faery Wicca is more of an umbrella term than a tradition in its own right. It refers to an element of the belief systems of several different paths within the Craft, which is the incorporation of fairy folklore and the active alignment with spirit entities called faeries (also spelled "fairies"). These beings can take a multitude of forms depending on the traditions they come from, but are often depicted as resembling humans.

Although faeries are most often associated with Celtic culture, they are not limited to this realm—belief in spirits that we would translate as "faeries" exists in ancient and contemporary cultures all over the globe.

In the English-speaking Faery traditions, they tend to be collectively referred to as "the fey." These earth-spirits are often associated with forests and hilly landscapes, and retain a surprisingly active presence in local folklore in rural Ireland and Scotland.

Wiccans who practice a Faery faith may call on these beings during spellwork, but there is a range of opinion on what kinds of magical aims faeries can be counted on to assist with.

Their personalities are generally not considered to be necessarily friendly toward humans (indeed, Peter Pan's Tinkerbell is pretty much an exception to the rule), although this can depend on circumstances, including whether or not the practitioner has offered or said something to get the fairies "on their side."

For example, it is believed that you can plant a garden or leave out items that will attract certain sprites into your yard or home. Because of the emphasis on working with spirits, Faerie Wicca is considered to be among the more shamanic practices on the Wiccan spectrum. Those who work this type of magic often work with oils, herbs, flowers, and other tools directly sourced from nature.

Faery Wicca is not the same as the Feri Tradition of witchcraft, which is a non-Wiccan form of the Craft developed in the mid-20th century in the United States by Victor and Cora Anderson. In fact, their tradition was initially called the Faery Tradition, but they changed the spelling to "Feri" in order to avoid being confused with the ever-growing number of Wiccan and other NeoPagan groups using the word "Faery" (or "Fairy") to identify themselves.

PART THREE

ECLECTIC WICCA

INTRODUCTION TO ECLECTIC WICCA

As you can see, there is quite a variety of potential paths for Wiccans to follow, whether they are solitary practitioners or initiates in a coven.

Ever since the days of Gardner and his first initiated witches, followers of the Craft have been innovating and adapting their practices to better suit their circumstances, their areas of interest, and their inner spiritual compasses, effectively creating new multiple traditions with each generation of Wiccans. And now that the phenomenon of solitary practice has become such a mainstay, it's become very common for individual Wiccans to create their own unique practices out of a sort of "patchwork" of many traditions, while also adding elements of their own invention.

Indeed, you could almost call "Eclecticism" its own "tradition" within Wicca, except that the only thing eclectic practices truly have in common with each other is that they're different from every other practice. In other words, the only tradition of eclecticism is independent thought and a willingness to be a spiritual pioneer, forging one's own path to a unique Wiccan practice.

The degree to which eclectic Wiccans "invent" their form of the religion (and not all Wiccans in this category would even necessarily agree with the term "religion") depends on the individual. Some might create highly unique ritual structures completely from their own inspiration and imagination, while others might simply blend Gardnerian and Dianic approaches, with little to no original material added in.

So you can see why it's essentially impossible to provide any specific information about the practice of eclecticism.

ECLECTIC SOLITARY PRACTICE

It's fair to say that the vast majority of eclectic Wiccans are solitary practitioners.

As discussed earlier, when you're practicing solo, you have the ultimate say in which direction, or directions, you'd like to explore along your spiritual path. While many solitaries do, in fact, choose to follow one specific tradition, it's probably the case by now that a majority of solitaries are eclectic in their practice.

One possible reason for this ever-rising trend is the wonderful diversity of perspectives offered in print and online sources about Wicca.

Solitary readers with no local Wiccan community to participate in are left with no other choice but to read, and (ideally) read widely, and in doing so, will find differing, and even conflicting, ideas about Wiccan philosophy, beliefs, and elements of ritual practice.

After some amount of initial exploration in this way, a solitary aspiring Wiccan will likely either feel drawn to a particular tradition and therefore keep pursuing sources that are part of that tradition, or feel somewhat uncertain about how to proceed. Those who feel uncertain will continue to read widely, and more likely than not, will cobble their own "traditions" together for themselves, with the help of the sources they resonate best with.

Another potential motivator for pursuing an eclectic path is the deity aspect of Wicca.

It can be a real stretch for those new to the faith, and particularly for those who were raised in one of the monotheistic religions (particularly Christianity) to suddenly be able to believe in a pagan deity from Greece or Egypt or Ireland who has, up until this point in their lives, been only a mythical character in stories, or else entirely unheard of.

Eclectic Wiccans can take a more gradual, individualized approach to the issue of deity. Perhaps the more generalized Goddess and God are easier for some to wrap their minds around. Or, perhaps there are one or two specific deities that make particular spiritual sense for a would-be traditionalist, but that aren't recognized by any traditions.

It's often said that relationships with deities must be cultivated over time—that you can't just automatically start believing in Isis just because your High Priestess insists that Isis exists. In eclectic practice, there's more room for forging one's own sense of what it means to worship a deity, and to come up with one's own language for describing it.

Of course, with eclectic solitary practice comes the challenge of essentially having to be your own teacher. You can read all you like—and you should—but at the end of the day, there's no one to guide you to your next step, because you're truly forging your own path.

Thankfully, we now have the possibility of virtual community via the Internet, and there's no shortage of people blogging, commenting, and otherwise chatting away about all things Wiccan, so you don't have to be completely solo if you don't want to be.

But if you're not following a specific tradition, then you have many, many more decisions to make on your own, and for some people, this gets overwhelming.

The best thing to do, if you're just starting out and you're unsure, is to read as much as you can, paying attention to what resonates with you as you do so, and let your heart lead you to the next step along the path.

ECLECTIC COVENS

It may almost seem like an oxymoron, but eclectic covens do exist.

After all, not all Wiccans who wish to be eclectic in their practice also wish to be solitary. An eclectic coven can be a wonderful place to find like-minded, independent spiritual companions with enough in common to make a well-functioning, diverse religious community.

The degree of uniqueness in any given eclectic coven will depend on why and how the coven was formed. For example, groups falling in this category may form because they believe in a blended cosmology—specific deities from a number of different pantheons—that don't fit neatly with any existing tradition. Beyond the deities of choice, the practice of such a coven may very closely emulate one of the more established traditions, but the more orthodox followers of that tradition will view the coven following a blended cosmology as "eclectic."

Other covens will deviate further from an existing tradition by merging it more extensively with another tradition.

While every single detail of the practice may belong to one of the established traditions, the fact that they are mixed together makes the coven "eclectic" rather than traditional.

Interestingly, this is often how new traditions get started. For instance, both Algard and Georgian Wicca are blends of the Alexandrian and Gardnerian Traditions with other elements mixed in, and each now has several covens practicing under their names.

Sometimes the move into eclecticism is gradual, rather than decisively chosen. For example, over time, some covens gradually adapt their practice to the extent that they're really no longer adhering to the basic tenets of the tradition they started out under.

An example of this would be if a coven was originally following the Dianic Tradition but decided to allow men access to the coven, and/or elected to worship a God in addition to a Goddess. The tradition cannot be called Dianic anymore—in the original sense—because the veneration of the Goddess has been sublimated and men are allowed to access the faith. (As noted above, there are now covens who identify as Dianic but don't emphasize the feminine, but for the purpose of this example, we're talking about the original Dianic Tradition.)

Finally, there are some covens that are deliberately and wildly eclectic from the very start, encouraging a diversity of practices among their members, provided that all involved will hold a few basic tenets in common.

These basic tenets are usually about ethics—tolerance for other paths, harm to none, etc. Within these groups, subgroups may form that have enough in common to move off on their own and solidify their own new traditions. Again, this is in keeping with the overall nature of Wicca over time—constant adaptation, evolution, and growth.

ECLECTIC CIRCLES

As mentioned earlier in this guide, Wiccan circles tend to be eclectic by design.

The great thing about this is that solitaries wishing to join a circle can be followers of a tradition or eclectic, and it doesn't matter either way.

In fact, some circles function as study groups who will take turns exploring different traditions, offering opportunities to build an eclectic practice for those interested in doing so.

If you're leaning toward eclecticism as opposed to following a specific tradition, and looking to commune and practice with others at least some of the time, then a circle is likely to be the most practical option for you.

MAKING PEACE WITH TRADITION

The term "eclectic" has essentially come out of the need to recognize, within the Wiccan community, that there are those who are going to stick to tradition and those who are not.

As mentioned above, there are plenty of Gardnerian and Alexandrian initiates (as well as those initiated in Seax Wicca, Dianic Wicca, etc.) who do not believe that a Wiccan can be self-initiated or be a solely solitary practitioner. Their traditions are sacred to them and while they don't necessarily begrudge other people following their own paths, they do mind it when said people call their path "Wicca."

One term sometimes used to describe those who don't follow coven-centered Gardnerian or Alexandrian Wicca is "NeoWiccan."

This is somewhat similar to the use of "NeoPagan" to distinguish those who currently follow Pagan practices today from those who worshipped "pagan" deities in the first centuries of the rise of Christianity. The Pagan practices of today may be based on and inspired by what we know of earlier times, but they are definitely not the same.

In this sense, "NeoWiccan" is a fair analogy, since eclectics and solitaries are not, in fact, practicing what Gardner and Alex Sanders practiced with their covens. The main difference is that "original" paganism happened literally centuries ago, and original Wicca has been around for far less than a century.

Furthermore, as has been stated several times already in this guide, Wicca has always been a dynamic, ever-changing religion since the beginning—both Gardner and Sanders continually revised their covens' Books of Shadows, adapting their practices as they went along.

So, while "NeoWiccan" makes sense to some—and some practitioners are happy to adopt the label for themselves—the more commonly used term is "eclectic," as it speaks to the nature of the people who pursue this type of path.

FOLLOW YOUR HEART

Again, the great thing about Wicca is that no one can tell you that you must join a coven, that you must practice alone, or that you must (or must not) follow a specific tradition. You get to decide for yourself.

However, you should definitely give yourself plenty of time to make this choice, and you should always remain open to the possibility that your decision could change over time.

Becoming an eclectic Wiccan, with all the freedom that "eclectic" implies, can sound like an enticing prospect, and it can be a very rewarding path for some. But it is only with serious soul-searching and study that you will find your true path of practice, so don't rule out the other traditions and modes of worship simply because being an eclectic witch sounds like a walk in the park.

If anything, it can be more difficult, because of the above-mentioned lack of comprehensive guidance and training from other Wiccans. But for those who truly feel called to eclecticism, many people describe it as a very liberating, personal path of spirituality that is no less sacred than following a single tradition.

PART FOUR

FINDING YOUR PATH

THE NEXT STEPS

The scope of Wiccan practice is quite impressive when we look at all the various ways in which it is followed. But given all the choices, it might actually be more difficult these days for interested beginners to find their way forward.

The first thing to remember is that it will probably take a while before you find your comfort zone within the Craft.

The tradition within Wicca of studying for a year and a day before being eligible for initiation into a coven speaks to the depth of the learning process. (In fact, plenty of covens will tell you that you're not necessarily ready to make that leap after only a year and a day.)

So take your time. And in the meantime, here are some suggestions for how you might take your next steps.

READ, READ,
AND READ SOME MORE

Research is the best thing you can do in order to gain an informed sense of the Craft and where your path into it might be found.

You're already well on your way there if you're reading this book, and this is just the tip of the iceberg when it comes to print and online resources.

Look into the things that you do not understand. Pursue further anything that really catches your interest. When you come across something that doesn't give you a good feeling—a belief, a practice, a particular author's take on things—take note of it, and see if you can sort out why it doesn't resonate with you. Understanding what you don't want helps you clarify what it is you're truly looking for.

You should be prepared to read several books, and blogs, if you're so inclined, on the topic of Wicca in your early days, and you should also resolve to never stop learning about it.

STUDY THE TRADITIONS

One of the easiest ways to figure out which type of practice is best suited to you is through studying the main Wiccan traditions. Again, it can be a challenge to find specific, detailed information about rites and rituals, etc., due to the traditions many orthodox covens have about keeping their knowledge secret.

If approaching a traditional coven isn't possible or just isn't your cup of tea, look up the traditions online, read books about them, and notice how you feel about each of them when you learn what they are about and how they operate. (You might start at the very beginning with Gardner's work, High Magic's Aid.)

If you find that they are unappealing to you in some way, discard the notion of joining that specific tradition or worshiping that specific pantheon.

Again, the point of it all is having an informed opinion, and that's gained through researching Wicca and its different paths.

FINDING THE RIGHT CIRCLE OR COVEN

Finding the circles and covens that operate in your area can be pretty close to impossible if you have no clue where to look.

While covens not looking for new members are unlikely to advertise their existence, some circles and Pagan groups use local media to announce meetings, ritual gatherings, etc. There are also online communities, forums, blogs, etc. that feature lists of covens and circles.

If you do find a directory of covens online, it will likely show what tradition the coven practices and how to contact a member or the High Priestess if they're looking for new members.

RESOURCES FOR SOLITARY WITCHES

Solitary practitioners who are new to the craft and do not have the guidance of other witches in their daily lives have to work a bit harder to find information.

In the Internet age, however, this is much less of a problem.

There are now countless resources out there for solo witches seeking guidance with spell-casting, rituals, and any other aspect of the faith. And, perhaps best of all, books can be ordered and delivered to those who don't have the luck to live in a community where such books might be sold.

Online Articles, Blogs, Videos, etc.

The Internet has indeed made it possible for the Wiccan community to be literally global.

There is probably no aspect of any tradition that hasn't been discussed online, and the diversity of voices from all over the world on any number of topics is truly astonishing.

There are some great blogs out there, and online videos can be wonderful resources for those who want to get closer to hands-on experience with ritual, etc. It's amazing what a good session with a search engine can do.

Of course, there's also a bunch of nonsense out there (this is the Internet we're talking about here, after all). There are writers with varying degrees of knowledge about their subject, and plagiarism runs rampant across many, many websites.

For example, one page on Wikipedia may be incredibly thorough, fact-checked, and well-written, while another on a related topic might be full of factual errors, or even completely made-up.

However, it's also fair to say that what constitutes "nonsense" to some will be perfectly legitimate and correct to others, and reading various sides of debates about traditionalism, etc. can be very insightful. But be a discerning reader, and evaluate your sources wisely.

If you're looking for a good starting point, I have just released my own website at **wiccaliving.com**. I also strongly recommend the excellent Celtic Connection resource, found at **Wicca.com**.

Online Forums and Message Boards

Online message boards, forums, and chat rooms can be a wonderful place to network with other Wiccans both in covens and outside of them. (And yes, there are even online covens!)

As mentioned above, these are excellent places to find out about covens and circles in your area and places near your location where there are meet-ups, but they also have great tips for ordering from online stores selling magical items and ritual tools, as well as general pleasant banter with like-minded folks.

Magazines and Newsletters

There have been magazines and newsletters on the Craft for decades and they're still, believe it or not, in existence.

Most are online now, offering websites with monthly or weekly updates and monthly newsletters via email, but print is not dead, so keep an eye out for the possibility of finding actual hard copies.

Books

Ah, good old-fashioned books.

Yes, books can still be the most comprehensive and focused resources for students of Wicca.

The best thing you can do to learn your Craft is amass a large collection of books on pantheons, traditions, spells, and magical correspondences.

One note to keep in mind here is that, like Internet sources, not all books are written by people with a solid education in the Craft. In the age of self-publishing, it's useful to check out whether a book has been published through a traditional publishing house, as those authors tend to be well-vetted and respected in the Wiccan community.

This doesn't mean that all self-published books are rubbish—some can be quite informative—but there is more of an issue of quality control.

CONCLUSION

By now, you should have a basic grasp of the myriad traditions and applications of Wiccan practice. If you're interested in pursuing the Craft further, the next recommended step is—as you may have guessed—to keep reading!

Find as many resources as you can, both in print and online, and dive into what interests you. Remember that there is no certified "correct" path into Wicca. If you want to follow an established tradition, you will find resources to get you started. If you favor an eclectic practice, the possibilities are virtually endless.

If you're interested in socializing with other Wiccans, another possible next step is to investigate potential circles or covens in your area. If you find the right group of people, this can be a wonderful way to enter the Craft, and it will almost certainly accelerate your pace of learning.

Of course, if you have friends who have a budding interest in Wicca as well, you can always form a "beginner's" circle in which you can study and learn together. For that matter, you can start a circle of your own by posting an inquiry in a suitable local publication, or in an online forum.

As noted earlier, it is important to keep your wits about you when it comes to group worship activities with people you don't know well. This is particularly true for covens, but it's good advice for circles also.

Don't ever let any kind of social pressure cause you to stay in a situation you find uncomfortable, and don't hesitate to walk away from illegal or potentially harmful activities. Again, these instances are rare, but they are possible due to the powerful energy inherent in the Craft and its appeal to certain less-than-stable personalities.

Of course, it's not just the rare instance of dodgy ulterior motives on the part of some who purport to be Wiccans that you should be on the lookout for. Pay attention to how the group energy feels, socially, as well. If you don't see yourself getting along well with one or more members of the group, then it might be pretty hard to relax into the learning and growth that these organizations are supposed to be providing.

Granted, most people take some getting used to, so don't dismiss a potential opportunity based solely on first impressions (unless the impression is really strong). Give others a chance, remembering that all friendships take time, while also being sure to be true to yourself.

As I always repeat at the end of my books: With Wicca, there is no right or wrong. This is especially true when you have such a diverse set of paths before you, and no one path is "better" than another. Indeed, the most important thing that you can do when seeking your path to travel is to follow your intuition. If, as you learn about a specific tradition, its philosophies and tenets and feel that it resonates deep within your heart, you're home.

If, on the other hand, you notice any little red flags coming up for you, pay attention to them. Spirituality should feel good in your whole being. If ritual feels like a chore, or something feels "off" in any other way, you're not quite in the right place.

Finally, remember that finding your path is bound to take some time. Adopting any new religion requires plenty of study and consideration, so don't be concerned if it takes several months or longer for you to feel you've started to get your footing. And even should you decide to become an initiate, whether through coven or solitary practice, you should never stop seeking new knowledge.

I will leave you with that parting thought. It has been an absolute pleasure writing this book, and I hope you have enjoyed reading it. I wish you all the best on your journey, whichever route you take, and I hope that you find your practice rewarding.

Thank you one more time for reading. Blessed Be.

SUGGESTIONS FOR
FURTHER READING

As emphasized several times throughout this guide, those who want to become Wiccans need to be willing to study the Craft extensively. This study ideally goes on throughout your life as a Wiccan, but you will find that reading as much as you can at the beginning will help you get a solid grounding in the many traditions, beliefs, and practices of Wicca.

Below is a very brief list of recommended books that beginners will find accessible. Information about covens, solitary practice, and many of the Wiccan traditions covered in this guide can be found in one or more of these resources, along with many other topics. You can find these books online and in Wiccan, Pagan, or other "New Age" shops. Happy reading!

Scott Cunningham, *Wicca: A Guide for the Solitary Practitioner* (1989)

Raymond Buckland, *Buckland's Complete Book of Witchcraft* (1986)

Gary Cantrell, *Wiccan Beliefs & Practices: With Rituals for Solitaries & Covens* (2001)

Phyllis Currott, *Witch Crafting* (2001)

Gerald Garner, *Witchcraft Today* (1954, 2004)

WICCA

LIVING A
MAGICAL LIFE

A Guide to Initiation and
Navigating Your Journey in the Craft

LISA CHAMBERLAIN

CONTENTS

INTRODUCTION

Whether it's due to the strong connection to the natural world, the enchanting mysteries of magic, or the sense of reconnecting to the ancient deities of pre-Christian times, people from all walks of life have found themselves drawn to learning more about what is commonly referred to as "the Craft."

For some, this interest is a passing fancy, or simply one of many destinations on a lifelong itinerary of spiritual exploration. Others instantly recognize the Craft as the obvious answer to something they've been searching for their whole lives, and never waver in their passion and enthusiasm for pursuing this spiritual path.

Still others fall somewhere in between. They feel called, somehow, to Witchcraft, but they're not quite sure what to do about it. They may "dabble" in nature worship and magic when they feel so inspired, but remain stalled when it comes to truly adopting the Craft as a way of life.

If you're reading this book, odds are that Witchcraft is more than a temporary interest for you, even if you're unsure about what your interest means. You're also likely to have wondered about how to formalize your commitment to the Craft—known in Witchcraft circles as "*initiation*". But what does that really mean?

Traditionally, initiation was associated purely with covens. In the first few decades of the rise of modern Witchcraft, covens were really the only option for learning and practicing what became known as "the Old Religion." One had to be initiated into a coven to fully access all of the knowledge its members held, and usually had to take an oath of secrecy so that the teachings and practices remained hidden from outsiders.

These days, of course, anyone can learn about and practice the Craft on their own, in a uniquely personal way. Some still assert that you can only be a "Witch" if you've been initiated by another, already-initiated Witch in a formal ceremony, but this is only true in covens following a traditional path like Gardnerian Wicca.

Outside of coven practices, there is no barrier to entry into this rich and diverse way of life. Those who practice solitary and eclectic forms embrace other kinds of initiation, which may or may not involve an actual ritual. And anyway, no one holds the power to determine whether another person is entitled to identify as a Witch—this decision is up to each individual.

Self-initiation (often called self-dedication) is now a widespread and respected tradition among Wiccans and other Witches, and can be a very affirming, and even life-changing experience.

It's an act of declaration to the Universe that you fully embrace your belief and participation in the Craft. It's an affirmation of your continued exploration and learning, and of your welcoming the blessing and assistance of the gods, the spirits, the energy, or however you describe your relationship with the seen and unseen manifestations of All That Is.

So how do you decide whether to formally enact this milestone? It's really up to you, but it's highly advisable to take your time and learn as much as you can about the Craft, until you're really getting a feel for your own personal path.

Initiation doesn't mean anything if you don't yet have a clue what you're doing, regardless of how interested you may be. A ritual is not going to suddenly catapult you into a full-blown magical existence, or guarantee that you'll stay on this particular path forever.

Throughout your life, it will be up to you to continue choosing the path, in your own way and at your own pace. You may initiate into one tradition but then decide to explore others. You may self-dedicate to the path you've been discovering, but end up practicing years later in an entirely different way, from an enhanced perspective that you can only gain over time. You may even ultimately decide to join magical forces with others in a coven of compatible fellow Witches.

Really, initiation can be a range of experiences—many solitary Witches describe being "initiated by the gods" in an unplanned, unexpected way, through signs or signals, epiphanies, or other experiences of communion with the unseen. This can occur as a single event or a series of them. Some Witches are gradually "initiated" over time, as their practice continues to deepen. Others might experience successive "initiation" events throughout their lives.

Indeed, even if you never undertake an initiation or self-dedication ritual, this doesn't mean you can't be a Witch—only you know who you really are.

This guide can be of use as part of your study as you make your way toward self-initiation or self-dedication, and will include further discussion of these options, along with an example ritual you can follow or adapt to suit your preferences. But the information here is intended to be valuable regardless of whether you choose a formal entrance into the Craft.

First, we'll examine some of the potential obstacles to stepping fully and decisively onto the path, and offer possibilities for moving past them. Then we'll take a look at the basic characteristics of the initiation process in both traditional covens and solitary forms of Witchcraft. Finally, we'll close with some ideas for integrating the practice of your path more fully into your daily life.

So whether you're just beginning to learn about Witchcraft, or have been "dabbling" for some time without quite finding a solid footing, you'll find something in this guide to aid you on your way. As you read, please keep an open mind, while staying in touch with your intuition. And as with any other spiritual resource, take what you need and leave the rest.

Blessed Be.

PART ONE

FINDING YOUR WAY

WALKING YOUR PATH

The word "path" is often used in reference to religion and spirituality, whether the subject is Christianity, Buddhism, Paganism, or any number of contemporary "New Age" belief systems. A person doing any kind of spiritual seeking is said to be "on the path" of that particular pursuit, whether it involves sitting in a church, meditating in a sanctuary, practicing yoga, lighting a candle, or reading a book.

This choice of phrase, "the path," is interesting.

It is not a *road*, which exists merely to get us from one place to another as quickly as possible, and where we can be slowed down, stopped, or rushed forward by the traffic of other people making their way toward their own destinations. It is a *path*, that winds and meanders in various directions in a quiet, leisurely way, allowing us to observe our surroundings at our own pace, unhurried and unimpeded by others.

On a path, the journey is completely our own, and there is no end-goal of a particular destination. The journey *is* the destination, and therefore we are always in the right place, even when it doesn't particularly feel like it.

"The path" is a good metaphor for the study and practice of Witchcraft, as it brings to mind images of walking in nature, whether the path leads through a forest, over the crest of a mountain, through a patch of desert, or along a vast, open stretch of coastline.

When we walk on a literal, physical path, our feet are on the ground, connected to the Earth. We are breathing fresh air and moving our bodies, interacting with the energies of nature. We feel alive and awake, and open to new discoveries around every bend. We can take note of the presence of animals, insects, clouds, breezes, sunshine, rocks, leaves, the sound of water rushing along a stream or of bird calls from the tallest branches of trees.

Likewise, as we advance along our path in the Craft, we can begin to interpret what we see, hear, feel and smell in the natural world as messages to our inner selves.

We have an inherent sense that we are part of something much larger than ourselves, something more significant than the small worries and annoyances of daily life. We have gratitude for being in the moment we're in, and a pleasant sense of expectation that the next moment will also be a good moment.

This is a great state of mind to be in, because it puts us in a perfect place to manifest positive experiences in our lives. In other words, we're poised to work some excellent magic. If only we could be in this state all the time!

The truth is, we can get there much more often than we think, even if we don't currently have the ability to take leisurely hikes through nature on a regular basis. We can still find these moments on our individual paths in our ordinary daily lives.

When we allow our lives to work with the natural rhythms of the Universe, pay attention to signs and signals, and maintain a practice of tending to our spiritual selves, we are walking our path. We are learning and growing from every experience, and deepening our understanding of, and ability to work successfully with, the powerful and magical energies of nature.

Sounds inspiring, doesn't it? And yet, this path can be really elusive at times.

COMMON CHALLENGES FOR ASPIRING WITCHES

For many beginning Witches, and even for plenty of those who have been practicing for years, the sense of being on a spiritual path can seem impossible to access in the midst of the hustle and bustle of modern life.

Studying and practicing the Craft is often relegated to the category of "leisure time," something to indulge in once the work day is over and all of the chores are done. For those who have initiation or self-dedication as a goal, it may seem like there's never enough time or energy for truly engaging in sufficient study. And even for those who aren't working toward a particular benchmark like initiation, finding the motivation to keep learning and practicing can still be a challenge.

So what can you do, if you're feeling yourself to be in a stuck place regarding your own path? The first thing to do is recognize that it's okay to be stuck.

Getting frustrated with yourself over where you are is never helpful—the energy of frustration doesn't manifest positive change. Not only does it keep you stuck, but it actually deepens the ruts that your "wheels" are spinning in.

So if you feel yourself to be stuck in a rut with your wheels spinning, then the first thing to do is get out of the car. It's not a road, remember? It's a path. Your path.

You're the only one on it, so you can stop whenever you want to, or need to—for as long as you want or need to. And you can trust that when you're ready, you'll resume walking at your own pace.

You can also remind yourself that plenty of people struggle with their paths—in fact, there's not a Witch in history who hasn't experienced some kind of block within their practice, for one reason or another.

Many people would argue that the whole point of being human is to experience obstacles and then grow by either overcoming them or learning to work with them. Witches can certainly be said to have an edge when it comes to navigating obstacles through the use of magic, but we all face difficulties, regardless of spiritual orientation.

Below, we'll take a look at some of the common challenges that would-be adept Witches encounter when it comes to moving beyond the mere reading of books and into the actual practice of the Craft. You'll also find some suggestions for navigating these challenges so you can continue to move along your path, at your own desired pace.

INFORMATION OVERLOAD

The first potential obstacle, ironic though it may seem, is the unprecedented amount of information about Witchcraft for anyone interested in the subject to take advantage of. Websites, books, magazines, videos, podcasts—you name it, it's out there.

In addition to the sheer volume, the *variety* of information can also be astonishing, since under the umbrella term of "Witchcraft" there are several distinctly different branches, including Wicca and its many different traditions, various forms of Traditional Witchcraft, and all kinds of eclectic practices that borrow from several older traditions at once.

And as a result of the dramatic rise in popularity of Wicca and Witchcraft in general in recent decades, new forms of the Craft are emerging all the time, generating still more new information. It really can be quite overwhelming.

In fact, some people who want to explore this territory find the vast scope of possible choices to be too much, unable to settle on a starting point. Others might spend some time collecting a shelf full of books on Witchcraft and other occult topics, and maybe even acquire a few magical tools, but find themselves unsure about their choices, and therefore unable to really "get into it" when it comes to developing a regular practice.

And then there's the related issue of conflicting information. Many aspiring Witches can get stuck when two or more sources they really respect describe vastly different approaches to a particular element of practice, such as how to begin a ritual. Indeed, it seems that one of the very qualities that draws many to the world of the Craft—the lack of rigid structures or uniform, standard procedures—can also be a challenge when it comes to finding your way in.

The good news is that most people who are interested in Witchcraft tend to be independent thinkers and have a strong connection to their own intuition. These traits can serve you well when it comes to navigating the maze of voices, perspectives, ideas and assertions that you're bound to encounter when researching the Craft.

The more you pay attention to your intuitive responses to what you read or hear—including emotional and physical responses—the more quickly you learn to discern between ideas that resonate and information that, for whatever reason, just doesn't speak to you.

So no matter how new you are to the subject of Witchcraft, remember to trust your own judgement and the signals that your higher self sends you. Read the books and websites that catch your interest, and give a pass to those that don't.

It's true that as you're setting out on your journey, you should read about a variety of perspectives and possible pathways, whether it be Wicca or other forms of Witchcraft—or both. But you can't possibly read everything, so don't exhaust yourself trying.

And don't ever feel obligated to take on another person's perspective on the Craft simply because they're emphatic about it. You may not have the level of experience that the author of a book or website has—you may, in fact, have none at all—but you are still the ultimate authority on your individual path.

LIVING AMONG
THE UNENLIGHTENED

In addition to being independent thinkers with a strong sense of intuition, people who are drawn to Witchcraft tend to have other traits in common, like an affinity with the natural world that goes beyond simply enjoying a hike and taking photographs of wildlife. They feel a sense of communion with nature when they're in it, a presence that isn't felt in the "civilized" world of suburbs and shopping malls.

Witches have a healthy appreciation of mystery, and enjoy contemplating phenomena that can't be understood through the lens of rational thought. They are at home with the feeling that there is much more to life than what is visible on the surface, that what constitutes "reality" goes well beyond everything we've been taught in our schools and our communities.

Finally, Witches tend to have unusually sharp sixth-sense (or "psychic") capabilities, whether these talents show up as clairvoyance (picking up spiritual messages through visual images), clairaudience ("hearing" messages from spirit as an inner voice), or empathy (tuning into the feelings of others).

Often, a person will have a combination of two or more of these gifts, but one may be dominant. These abilities allow us to "just know" things without any tangible evidence, and when we recognize and trust them, they help us make good decisions and avoid trouble.

It probably goes without saying that these characteristics are not exactly prized in mainstream culture.

Although it's true that independent thinking (or "thinking outside of the box") is considered a positive attribute in the workplace in many fields, our social worlds—particularly in the United States—still overwhelmingly favor compliance with the dominant belief systems at work in our culture, whether these come from science-based "rational" thinking, one of the major world religions, or a mix of both.

In this environment, psychic abilities and a fascination with the unseen are met with suspicion, rather than enthusiasm. "Witchy types" may feel out of their element most of the time, and are unlikely to feel

166

safe sharing their own worldview and experiences with the people around them.

Indeed, despite the above-mentioned explosion of interest in the subject over the past few decades, Witchcraft remains incredibly taboo in the majority of the English-speaking countries in which it's practiced.

Even (and perhaps especially) in the U.S., where Wicca has actually been granted official status as a religion, identifying publicly as a Witch can be incredibly risky, depending on where you live. People who are uneducated about the Craft may accuse you of "devil-worship," suspect you of illegal drug use, or decide that you must be mentally unstable.

So if you don't have any friends or family members who share your interest, or are at least tolerant of it, you may be keeping this very significant aspect of your life a total secret, with no one at all to discuss it with. It can feel a bit lonely at times, to say the least.

Of course, not everyone is in this situation. If you live in a cosmopolitan city where attitudes are liberal and "anything goes," or if you at least have friends or acquaintances in your community who share your interests, then you most likely don't have to be closeted about your identity as a Witch.

Or, you may be one of those rare people who just has absolutely no hangups whatsoever about what other people think. Perhaps you play the role of a trailblazer for the Craft in your community, using your courage and inner strength to openly pave the way for others to come out of the shadows, in which case, you are much appreciated by your fellow Witches!

But if you, like most humans, prefer as much harmony in your social and/or family life as possible, you may find that you're better off not disclosing your identity as a Witch. There's nothing wrong with this at all, but many find that it does make it a bit hard to maintain enthusiasm for consistent study and practice.

The good news is that even if you're not blessed with the presence of like-minded others in your life, there are a few things you can do to energize your desire to keep moving forward on your path.

First, know that there's really no *need* to be "out" as a Witch to anyone in your life. In fact, many traditions of Witchcraft require vows of secrecy, whether to avoid social ostracism or to honor those who came before us in prior centuries, when being known as a Witch was a very real threat to one's safety, and could even cost people their lives.

So even if you're completely solitary on your path, you're actually still in good company. And of course, on the astral plane, you're never truly alone—you can always communicate with those in the spirit world who support you in your pursuit of the Craft.

Second, you can take advantage of living in the Internet Age and do some research to find out whether there are like-minded people in your area. It's entirely possible that there are others who feel the same way you do about maintaining secrecy in the outer world, but still would like to communicate with other Witches in private. This could be in the form of a coven, or something more informal like a circle or discussion group.

And even if there's no one to meet with in person for hundreds of miles, there are definitely plenty of online groups—particularly among Wiccans, but also among other Witches—where you can connect, ask questions, share ideas, and find camaraderie with others who share your solitary plight.

Finally, the most important step—no matter what your social circumstances may be—is to own and embrace who you really are. If you feel called to the Craft, answer that call, and let the connection it fosters with your true self be the most important thing in your life.

So many people who participate in the dominant, monotheistic religions are doing so at least partly out of a perceived social obligation. ("If I don't go to church, other people will notice and then gossip about me!") In fact, so many people never get in touch with who they really are on any level, because they're too busy trying to conform to the expectations of mainstream society.

Viewed in this light, the path of the solitary, secretive Witch is perhaps the most incredibly freeing and self-validating spiritual experience available to you. After all, you're definitely not doing this for anyone but yourself!

As it happens, when you embrace your witchy self just as you are, and don't allow social or cultural prejudices to get in your way, you are much more likely to attract new people into your life who resonate with your spirituality, your personality, and your way of perceiving the world.

So focus on you and your own growth, and live from your heart. As you progress along your path, you may eventually find that you've become comfortable sharing your spiritual side with more people, which will in turn attract more like-minded people to you.

In fact, we've been seeing this phenomenon in the exponential growth of practitioners of the Craft over the past few decades. As new generations have discovered the path, we have collectively made major advances in acceptance of, and even respect for, this beautiful and creative way of life.

So be proud of your path, and of yourself for following it, regardless of whether you'd ever tell anyone in your life what you're up to.

SO MANY MOONS, SO LITTLE TIME...

Another challenge that new Witches may struggle with is not quite knowing how to integrate their spiritual and magical practice into the daily routines of their otherwise-mundane lives.

If you work 40 (or more) hours per week, or are in school, or have the responsibility of taking care of a family (or all of the above), it can be hard to feel that you even have time for reading about the Craft or engaging in a little spellwork, let alone observing the 13 full moons and 8 sabbats on the Wheel of the Year.

And if you're a solitary Witch, with no coven or circle to celebrate moons and holidays with, it can be harder to summon up the motivation to clear your calendar and devote your time and attention to these special days.

You may even find yourself putting off spellwork that you know would be beneficial to your life, because you can't see how to get yourself in the right frame of mind to make it effective. It can be quite a feat to shake off the workday sludge and allow space for that magical feeling to flow through you.

If you're feeling dispirited about not being able to build spiritual activity into your life, it's important to recognize that you don't need to take an all-or-nothing approach. Remember, it's called a path for a reason—you're supposed to take it one step at a time, and you're supposed to go at your own pace.

There are no rules about how much, or how often, or when or where or in what way to practice your Craft. But there are many small, purposeful steps you can take toward your goal of creating a more regular, consistent practice.

First of all, keep in mind that unless you are a member of a Wiccan coven that operates through participation in scheduled rituals, there is no requirement that you observe all, or any, of the full moons, solstices, equinoxes, or other festivals associated with the Wheel of the Year. If you are following a Wiccan path, then these are definitely a big component of the spiritual life, but that doesn't mean that you're doing something wrong if you don't honor every single holiday.

These times exist as opportunities to connect with the Earth, with any deities you may work with, and with the spirit energy of other Witches following a similar path in their own way. But they should be seen as opportunities rather than obligations. Whether you're practicing Wicca or some other path of the Craft, if you're going about your preparations for a sabbat or full moon ritual and feeling stressed or even a little resentful about it, then something's not right.

To allow for a more relaxed and joyful approach to celebrating whatever holidays you're able to, embrace the art of compromise.

If the Spring Equinox is coming up and you see that it falls on that Wednesday when you have a late meeting after work, then you could choose to mark it on Thursday, or even Tuesday, instead. While it's fun, and often quite powerful, to perform a ritual as close to the exact time of an equinox as possible, it's not like there's a huge amount of difference in the length of day and night between Tuesday, Wednesday, and Thursday of that week.

In other words, these holidays mark *points* on the wheel of the seasons. The purpose of observing them is to acknowledge where we are on the wheel at that time. A few days on either side of that designated point is not going to diminish the power of your intentions. You're still taking time to focus on the present moment and be in gratitude for the blessings in your life.

Of course, when it comes to timing celebrations of full and new moons, there's a little less leeway, given that the lunar cycle is so much shorter than the solar cycle. Nonetheless, if you're wanting to work some full moon magic but can't time it exactly right, go ahead and do it the night before!

If your intention is just as clear and strong as it would be on the actual night of the full moon, there's no reason to believe you won't be successful. Most people feel the energetic effects of a full moon for at least two or three days surrounding the moment when it's technically full, so why would magic only be potent at that specific time?

That's not to say that certain spells that are *designed* for exact timing with the full moon can be worked whenever you want and turn out successfully—timing is a magical tool, after all. But you can choose spellwork that isn't targeted for a specific point in time. And remember that magic has been around since long before most people had the ability to know the exact moment of a moon phase by checking their clocks. So don't put off spellwork that you really want to do simply because you can't do it at the "perfect" time.

Speaking of timing, another way of integrating Witchcraft more fully into your life is to observe the various magical correspondences between moon phases, as well as days of the week, and specific purposes.

It's generally understood that spells worked for increase (in terms of prosperity or love, for example) are best done when the moon is waxing or full, while spells worked to remove something from your life (an illness, a debt, or some other unwanted situation) are best during the waning phase.

To get even more specific, each day of the week has its ideal magical goals, based on the planet assigned to the day. Friday, associated with Venus, is the first choice for love spells, while Thursday, ruled by expansive Jupiter, is good for magic relating to money and prosperity.

If you put both of these systems together, then you can see that a Friday during a waxing moon would be the best time to work a spell for attracting a new relationship. A Thursday during a waning moon is good for spellwork to eliminate obstacles to prosperity.

Some Witches find the daily correspondences and the moon phase considerations to be too restrictive. After all, what if you have an urgent communication-related need that you want to perform spellwork for, that isn't going to wait until two Wednesdays from now when the moon is waxing again? In fact, plenty of non-Wiccan Witches ignore the daily correspondences altogether—although most do work with the moon phases.

The truth is, you should do your spellwork when you're able and willing to, regardless of the day of the week. As always, your focus on your intention is the single most important factor in any magical working. But it's good to recognize that daily correspondences and moon phases offer opportunities to work some structure into your magical practice.

Say a sudden inspiration to do a candle spell strikes you one evening, but you feel overwhelmed by the possibilities for a specific intention. You can use the correspondences to help you decide!

If it's Saturday, and the moon is waxing, you might choose to work for increased psychic clarity. Now you've narrowed it down to a specific goal, and you know that your work for this goal has the support of the moon and the planet Saturn. And just knowing this brings an extra magical boost to your work!

Ultimately, integrating the Craft into your daily life—one step at a time, at your own pace—is the goal. The sabbats and moon cycles create an ongoing, affirming rhythm in our lives around the Wheel of the Year, but it's in our daily habits—of mind and of practice—where lasting spiritual development occurs.

There are many small, yet significant ways to gradually transform your life so that you're living a magical experience every single day, whether or not you have time for elaborate spellwork. Let's take a look at some practices you can incorporate into your daily routine that will keep your magical connection with the Universe in your daily awareness.

First and foremost, if you don't do this already, consider adopting a daily meditation practice. Witches, sages, and mystics have known for centuries what modern brain science is just now discovering—that meditation creates very powerful, positive changes in the brain that can enhance our abilities to do just about anything, and this certainly includes magic!

We tend to get overrun, without even realizing it, by unnecessary and unhelpful thoughts zooming around in our busy minds from morning until night. Almost all of these thoughts are somehow related to something in our past or a concern about our future. A daily practice of meditation helps us get better at letting go of those thoughts, allowing us to focus on what's right in front of us, which is a key component of successful magic.

You probably already know that any spellwork performed with a distracted, sped-up, "monkey" mind is quite unlikely to be successful, which is why Witches take such care to achieve a clear, relaxed, focused state of mind before beginning any ritual or other magical work.

If you're in a regular habit of meditation, you have more familiarity with this state of mind, and can achieve it more quickly and easily when it comes time to engage with the Universe on a magical level. And simply *knowing* you can get there more easily is often enough to get you past that resistant voice that says "I'm too frazzled to focus enough for magic today."

This doesn't mean that you need to sit cross-legged in the lotus position chanting "om" on a cushion for 30 minutes a day (although you'd benefit enormously in many ways if you did so!). The goal here is to develop a practice that you can stick to, so start with an amount of time that you know is manageable, even if it's as little as 5 minutes.

You can play some soothing music or meditative sounds, or even a guided meditation—all of which can be found for free online. If you have a timer on your phone or an alarm clock, you can set it for the desired length of time, so that you won't have to open your eyes to see how long you've been at it. (Try to use something that makes a gentle sound when the mediation's over—it's rather jarring to be interrupted by loud beeps or other "alarming" alarm sounds!) You'll find more tips for successful meditation at the end of this section, along with a short, simple meditation to try.

Try to meditate around the same time every day, so that your body and mind get into a rhythm with it. Once you're in a groove, start adding one minute to your timer every week or so, in order to gradually increase the length of your meditations.

A meditation practice builds its own momentum over time, so you should begin to notice differences in your anxiety levels and ability to focus after a couple of weeks. You'll also notice that you feel you have more time to pay attention to your Craft, since slowing down and centering are key elements of working with the energies of the natural world.

There are other simple ways to infuse your daily life with a more magical awareness.

You can make charm bags with your favorite crystals, herbs, and/or other ingredients and keep them in various places where you'll see them each day—such as in your kitchen and your car. You can charge your morning coffee with an affirmation or blessing, setting a positive intention for the day and truly savoring that first magical sip. You can carry crystals in your pockets during the work day, and hold them during times of stress or boredom, keeping you in touch with the magical energies of the Earth.

Crystals and other mineral stones are also great in jewelry, of course, and this is a particularly good option for people who don't want their identities as Witches to be known to those around them. You can quite openly wear an amber pendant, charged for luck, protection, or some other magical purpose, and though you'll likely get plenty of compliments on it, no one will be the wiser!

Over time, working these small practices into your daily life will create a foundation for your spiritual evolution, and help ground and center you on your path.

As you continue to learn and grow in the Craft, remember that it does take time to build a deep personal practice, and that your pace is your own. As time goes on, you'll be able to look back at the early stages of your pursuit of this path and see how much more comfortable and confident you've become, little by little. And it's more than likely that as you relax about whether or not you're marking all the moons and holidays, you will find yourself with more time and energy to celebrate these occasions.

So resist any temptation you feel to be a perfectionist about "sticking to the schedule." Don't indulge in guilty feelings about skipping your morning meditation or letting a new moon go by without lighting a candle. Approach every ritual, celebration, and magical working you're able to devote time to with an attitude of ease and joy, and trust that you're exactly where you're supposed to be in every moment.

RELIGION AND RATIONALISM: GETTING BEYOND OLD BELIEFS

For some would-be Witches, the biggest hurdle to fully embracing a life in the Craft is not their social circumstances or their busy schedules. Instead, it's the challenge of reconciling the beliefs involved in practicing Witchcraft with whatever beliefs they were brought up with, whether those are religious, rationalist, or a mix of both.

These days, more and more Witches are born into families that already practice Wicca or some other form of the Craft, and therefore begin learning about it from an early age. However, this is not the case for the vast majority of people who find themselves drawn to this way of life.

Many aspiring Witches discover the Craft as teenagers. Others are young adults or even middle-aged adults. Those who remain interested in it after reading a few sources have found ideas or beliefs that resonate with them. But the process of accepting and adopting a new belief system can still feel unclear.

LOSING YOUR RELIGION

While it seems that a majority of Witches were raised in non-religious families, or else had parents who had left their own families' religion behind, many do come to the Craft from religious backgrounds. Most were brought up in a denomination of Christianity, but other faiths are represented as well.

A religious upbringing can be tricky for an aspiring Witch, particularly for those who grew disillusioned with a faith they once followed, and especially for those whose family lives were strongly infused with their religion.

If this is your situation, you might experience resistance to much of what you read and hear about Witchcraft, no matter how much it resonates with some parts of you. This resistance might be subtle or quite active, and can come from a variety ideas that you may have consciously let go of, but are deeply ingrained nonetheless.

For example, you might struggle with adopting a new concept of deity, such as the Wiccan God and Goddess, or any of their "lesser" aspects from the various pantheons that practitioners of Wicca and other forms of the Craft follow. You may have had it instilled in you from an early age that the deity (usually known simply as "God") of your religion is the only one, and that any other deity is completely fabricated by human beings, or else somehow inappropriate to give your attention to.

Many sects of Christianity in particular have long held that anything with the slightest whiff of paganism is inherently "evil," but this idea is found within the other monotheistic religions as well. So even though you know in your heart that there's nothing wrong with following a different deity, and doing so in an entirely different way, it can still feel rather strange.

You may also have been raised with a concept of deity (usually "God") as one who is both benevolent and punishing, watching and judging your every action and providing you with plenty of opportunities to feel guilty if you're not living up to what you've been taught is the ideal standard of behavior. In this kind of belief system, a rigid concept of the afterlife is often used as motivation for keeping oneself in line, and the rules involved can run from simple to complex, and from sensible to seemingly random and bizarre.

People who leave religions with strict dogma tend to be wary of the word "god," whether it's capitalized or not, and are generally resistant to anything resembling "rules." So when you come across a Witch or a book that appears to take a dogmatic approach to the Craft (such as a fixed arrangement of the altar that must be followed consistently, or some other element of practice that can only be viewed from a specific perspective), it can be off-putting.

The concept of goddesses is also challenging for some who have been raised in the patriarchal religious systems of Judaism, Christianity, and Islam, although this is also a major draw, if not *the* major draw, for many Witches who work with deities.

The presence of a divine feminine and the balanced equality between the two genders in many forms of the Craft is a refreshing and welcoming experience for many who come from a patriarchal background. And some forms of Wicca actually leave male deities out of it altogether. Nonetheless, if your former notion of divinity was exclusively male, then goddesses can be a little hard to get used to.

Not all forms of Witchcraft recognize deities, however, and it should also be acknowledged that a vast number of Witches would reject the idea that their path is a religion. Wicca is officially recognized as a religion in many places, but even some Wiccans decline to identify it that way.

It should also be noted that there are Witches who continue to practice their religion of origin along with Witchcraft and see no conflict between the two—even if most members of that religion of origin would disagree!

If you're feeling called to the Craft, but uncertain or hesitant about how the concept of deity fits with your worldview as a "religious refugee," know that your experience of this path is yours alone.

No one can make you believe in anything, and no amount of worshiping or honoring or invoking a deity is going to make it real for you if you're just going through the motions because it seems like you're "supposed to." Unless you belong to a Wiccan coven that worships particular aspects of the Goddess and God, you really have a wide range of possibilities to explore in this department.

If following a well-established path is what feels right, then you may be more predisposed to follow deities that are widely believed in by members of specific traditions. Or you can take the "eclectic" route and build your own practice, which may or may not include deities.

No matter how your path evolves, you can let go of the idea that any one religion or belief system is the "correct" one. In fact, it can be very useful to allow for the possibility that the infinite Universe has room for *all* deities and *all* beliefs, with no one particular set of ideas being any more correct than another.

You can also relax, take your time, and trust that you will find your way when you're ready. Although some people do end up having a specific mystical or spiritual experience that immediately opens them up to a new understanding of the non-physical world in a particular and lasting way, most of us come to an understanding of our deities of choice (or lack thereof) more gradually.

So don't let mixed feelings about "religion" stop you from following your inner guidance. Know that if you listen to yourself first, you'll always end up where you're meant to be.

THAT PESKY THING CALLED "PROOF"

As mentioned earlier, people who adopt Witchcraft as a way of life are more likely than not to have been raised in non-religious families. They might describe their upbringing as "atheist," "rationalist," or simply "not religious."

There's a spectrum of belief systems represented here, from those with staunchly atheist views, many of whom will *insist* that there is no "God," and that the deities of all cultures around the globe are simply human fabrications, to agnostics, who aren't completely sure either way. (Rationalists, like atheists, reject the notion of deity, but like agnostics, tend not to feel the need to actively "take a side" in the question.)

Rationalists, by definition, take a very skeptical attitude toward unseen phenomena, whether it be paranormal activity, magic, or anything else that can't be proven to be real by some acceptable scientific standard. Atheists may very well believe in the invisible realms, but dispute the notion that any kind of deity is responsible for aiding in magical manifestations.

Of course, depending on your personal perspective, these terms may overlap. Unlike organized religions, there's no creed for atheism or rationalism, other than a belief that deities do not exist, so there's no established definition of either. And there are other terms—like "skeptic" or "humanist"—that many non-religious people identify with instead.

There are, however, plenty of Witches who identify with any number of these terms.

Atheist Witches participate in the spirit realm and practice magic, but do not, obviously, work with deities.

Rationalist Witches practice magic, but don't subscribe to the "spiritual" worldview. Instead, they understand the power to manifest as a result of the psychological effects that spellwork creates in the brain, making them more likely to focus and make choices that lead them to their goals.

Or, they may understand it as a result of the Law of Attraction, a topic which has gained plenty of currency in the last several years, even among many in the mainstream culture. Then there's the cutting-edge field of quantum physics, which has been evolving to a point where its theories can essentially be viewed as the underpinnings of how magic works.

These concepts are generally easier for many aspiring Witches with "non-mystical" worldviews to wrap their minds around. Even so, when you're new to the Craft, it can take some time to get to a place where your skeptical origins can peacefully coexist with phenomena that can't be "proven" or explained in a traditional scientific manner.

Particularly given the culture we live in, which would essentially brand you as crazy for believing in magic, it can be hard to get beyond "keeping an open mind" to truly accepting the ideas underlying your new practice on a consistent basis.

If this is your situation, you may very likely experience fluctuating confidence about choosing this path. You may have brief glimmers of an unseen force moving through you and around you in a particularly magical moment, but then wake up the next day thinking it must have just been your imagination. And if you're keeping your explorations of Witchcraft a secret from family or friends in order to avoid awkward or even contentious conversations, it can be a lonely road to solidifying your beliefs.

The trouble with this dance between skepticism and acceptance, particularly when it comes to magic, is that without real belief, you *can't* make it work. And if the spellwork you're trying doesn't get results, it has the effect of reinforcing your doubt.

This kind of block can happen no matter what kind of beliefs were instilled in you from a young age— many, if not most people from religious backgrounds also struggle with resistance from their "rationalist" beliefs. Indeed, this is a place many, many aspiring Witches find themselves in at the beginning, and it's pretty easy to get stuck here, especially if you don't have the support of others in your life who have gotten past it.

So what can you do to move through this "agnostic" phase of your path?

First of all, it's key to have patience—again, frustration doesn't get you anywhere.

Second, stay open to the same perspective offered above to those who are inhibited by their former religious beliefs: there are many, many paths to understanding and consciously participating in the grand cosmic scheme of things.

As you continue to seek your own path, remember to take it one step at a time. Keep your spellwork simple, with relatively minor or short-term goals. Candle magic is a great form for beginners, particularly because it's hard to gaze on a flickering flame without being at least a little enchanted! Try a candle spell for elevating your mood—these often have especially notable results, which will last longer and longer the more you practice.

Meditating, spending time in nature, and "unplugging" from unnecessary stimuli like television and social media will always enhance your spiritual side.

And of course, keep reading everything you can about the Craft. Become more discerning about which authors and ideas resonate with you, and discard anything that doesn't. Finding a book or a blog or a website that inspires you is often just the thing you need to open up further and expand your understanding of your path.

No matter who you are or where you're from, you really do have to transform your ingrained and often unconscious beliefs in order to accommodate a life in the Craft. This is part of the work of initiation, whether you undergo a formal ritual or not.

It could be argued that teenagers have it the easiest in this regard, since it's in the nature of people at this stage in life to explore widely as they seek to shape their identities and their way of seeing the world. They're generally quite open to new ideas and alternative perspectives.

There's also an almost electrical charge to much of life at this age, which can make perceiving unseen realities much easier. This may be at least part of why Wicca and other forms of Witchcraft are so popular with teenagers and young adults.

By contrast, many people say that the older we get, the harder it is to be open to change and to shake off long-held beliefs about how the world works. However, this isn't necessarily true. It really all depends on your particular circumstances—your upbringing, your personality, the events of your life thus far, and your openness to change in general.

But whatever your age or background, your pursuit of the Craft shows that you're not much interested in sticking to a conventional way of viewing the world. Knowing this about yourself is a good start toward feeling at home in the magical and spiritual life you're now creating.

SPELLS AND PRACTICES FOR MORE MAGICAL LIVING

In some ways, it could be argued that "path" is not exactly a perfect metaphor for the experience of bringing the Craft into one's life.

"Path" rather implies that the ground you're walking on is well-tended, that there are no forks or detours or obstacles to interrupt your smooth stroll.

In truth, this quest is more like a "trail," where there may be narrow, rocky patches or fallen trees that must be climbed over, or forks that give no indication of where you'll end up once you've chosen one direction over another.

If your chief obstacle is choosing among the seemingly infinite possibilities of beliefs and forms within the umbrella term of "Witchcraft," it may feel like you're facing several different "forks" at once. Or, you could simply be feeling lonely out there, with no one in your family or social sphere to share your interest and discoveries with.

Maybe your challenge is in integrating the time and focus it takes to advance along the path into your busy life. Or perhaps it's about getting past old, limiting beliefs about the Universe and what we have been taught to identify as "reality."

In all actuality, it's likely that each of these circumstances will affect you to some degree, at some point or another, since they are such common elements of life in the 21st century.

Fortunately, none of these obstacles can actually force you off your path—only you can decide whether or not the Craft is really for you. And though patience and persistence are key to moving forward, there are also plenty of practical steps you can take to move out of places that feel "stuck."

You'll find some examples below, in the form of meditation ideas and a bit of spellwork. Try them out and see what works for you.

And no matter what you do, keep in mind that on nature hikes—particularly the wilder, more adventurous ones—the "path" can sometimes be very faint, or even seem to disappear altogether for awhile, before it becomes clear again.

When this happens to you, keep trusting that you're still on track, as you take those tentative steps in between the visible stretches.

"PROTECTIVE BUBBLE" ENCHANTMENT

When you're spending most of your time among the "unenlightened," the path can get pretty obscured at times.

Witches tend to be very sensitive to the energetic vibrations of the people around them. This is generally considered to be a blessing, and can be marvelous when you're surrounded by positive, open-minded people.

But most of us are not so blessed as to be in this situation at all times. And when you're around people who are negative or closed-minded, it's easy to be affected by their moods and lose your connection to your witchy inner self.

This is particularly true for Witches who work in occupations that are inherently stressful, fast-paced, and/or involve interacting with the public, but it can also be an issue in one's home environment as well.

This enchantment technique helps you keep healthy boundaries around your personal energy, shielding you from the negativity of others and keeping you connected to your own spiritual power. Best of all, you can draw upon it whenever you need to throughout your day without calling attention to the fact that you're working magic!

To set up the enchantment, you'll need some time and space where you can be alone and undisturbed. This is very important, since you are creating an energetic experience that you'll be relying on when you're in the midst of people who are difficult to be around.

In other words, you need to have a solid foundation of peace and well-being to draw from. So be sure to establish a feeling of calm and serenity before you begin, perhaps by using the Reconnection Meditation exercise described below.

This enchantment connects a physical gesture to a feeling of calm, centered well-being.

Instructions:

Choose a gesture you can make with your hand that's reasonably subtle and will not draw the attention of others.

This can be anything that comes naturally to you, but commonly used examples include making a circle with your thumb and index finger, crossing your fingers, or making a fist, all of which can be done when your arms are at your sides and your hands are out of view.

You can also try tugging gently at your earlobe, or placing your palm on the back of your neck. You may want to experiment a little until you find something you're comfortable with.

Once you've chosen your gesture, close your eyes and take three deep breaths, letting go of any extraneous thoughts or concerns.

Make the gesture, and as you do, envision yourself surrounded completely by a bubble of pure white light.

Hold this vision for several moments, allowing yourself to feel completely protected and at peace. No unwanted energy from others can disturb you in this place, and nothing can come between you and your spiritual center.

When you feel a very strong connection between this feeling and the gesture you're making, you can say the following affirmation, or create one of your own:

"All is right, bright and well here in my center."

Take another deep breath, release it, and then open your eyes.

Keep holding the gesture for another deep breath or two with your eyes open, to lock in the association between the gesture and the feeling. When you feel ready, you can then release the gesture.

You have now created a powerful, portable enchantment. The next time you're in a social situation of any kind that feels uncomfortable, you can subtly make your gesture, take a conscious, focused breath, and bring that bubble of protective light immediately to your assistance.

If you like, you can repeat the affirmation silently to yourself. The more you use this enchantment, the stronger and more instantly effective it will become.

QUICK "RECONNECTION" MEDITATION

As discussed above, a regular meditation practice is highly recommended for every Witch, but especially for those who have busy schedules, as a hectic pace of life can make it quite difficult to slow down and tune in to your inner self.

This very brief meditation exercise is useful at any point in the day, but particularly when you feel disconnected from yourself due to distractions caused by others, or by stressful circumstances. Try using it as a way of transitioning from the work day to the evening, especially when you're planning to work magic and/or celebrate a holiday.

This exercise is most effective when you're sitting comfortably in a quiet place, but you can also do it "on the go" just about anywhere you happen to be. The main thing is to be paying attention to your breathing throughout the meditation.

Instructions:

Close your eyes and take a long, slow, deep breath in as you (silently) count to four. Hold your breath for another count of four, and then gently, slowly, let it go, again to a count of four.

Then wait for another count of four before taking the second long, slow, deep breath in.

Hold for another count of four, let it go, and then wait one more count of four before opening your eyes and returning to breathing as normal.

Note that you don't have to stop after two rounds of this—you can do this exercise for as long as you like—but be sure to do at least two cycles of breathing in, holding, breathing out, and holding before opening your eyes.

When you finish, take a moment to notice how the difference in the "noise level" in your mind, as well as any other sensations that come through. You may want to close out the meditation with an affirmation, such as *I am now reconnected with my center*, or *Blessed Be*.

TIPS FOR THE MEDITATING WITCH

Although we generally think of meditation as an Eastern spiritual activity, there are plenty of ways to blend Western Witchcraft into your meditation practice.

You can surround yourself with crystals and/or light a candle to sit in front of during your meditation. You can also choose specific Tarot (or other divination) cards to hold and gaze at while you pay attention to your breath.

Some Witches like to concentrate on the card, then close their eyes and hold the imagery in their third eye for as long as they can. This helps slow down the "monkey mind" by providing it with a visual task.

If you have a patron deity, you can use an image of the deity in this manner as well, and in this way forge a stronger spiritual connection with the deity through your meditation.

Finally, incense or essential oils in a diffuser can enhance your mind's ability to slow down and enter an altered state. If you use incense, be sure to sit a good distance from the actual smoke so you don't inhale it as you breathe deeply.

If you've never meditated before, or if you've tried but found yourself unable to "stop thinking thoughts," don't worry!

In actuality, successful meditation does not have to be "thought-free." You will almost certainly get distracted by random, uninvited thoughts during meditation.

The trick is to let them go, rather than engaging with them. So any time you realize that you've drifted off into your to-do list again, or are replaying something that happened earlier in your day, simply let it go and return your focus to your breath.

Part of the magic of meditation is that simply *trying* to slow down your mind, no matter how successful (or unsuccessful) you are, makes a significant difference. So regardless of how distracted or scattered you're feeling as you start your meditation, know that it's never a waste of time or effort!

"SPIRIT CONNECTION" CHARM BAG

Charm bags are fun, easy ways to keep a little magic with you wherever you go. You can keep them discreetly in your pocket, wear them on a cord around your neck, or hang them over the rearview mirror of your car. If you have a desk job, try keeping one in a drawer that you use frequently.

The main thing is to keep your charm bag in a place where you'll see it on a daily basis. If you find, after some time has gone by, that you're not really noticing it anymore, then move it to a new location where it will catch your attention again.

You can find small, inexpensive drawstring bags made of cotton, silk, or muslin at most craft stores, or order them online. Alternatively, you can make a charm "bundle" with a piece of scrap cloth gathered up at the corners and tied with a ribbon.

You will need:

- 1 small drawstring bag
- 3 small crystals of your choice
- ¼ cup dried flowers and/or dried herbs of your choice
- 1 small square of paper (about 1 inch by 1 inch)
- Pencil (or pen) and/or markers or crayons
- 1 tea light or votive candle

Instructions:

This charm bag should be as personalized as possible. Choose stones and herbs that have spiritual significance for you. If you're new to crystals and/or herbs, here are some suggestions, all of which have associations with spiritual strength and development:

Crystals: amethyst, blue calcite, kyanite, malachite, moonstone, quartz crystal.

Herbs: basil, cinnamon, dandelion, lavender, mug, sage.

Note: If you prefer to use potpourri instead of individual herbs, try to go with an all- natural blend, as synthetic fragrances tend to be disruptive to personal energy.

Light the candle as you hold your intention to create a powerful talisman that will keep you connected to your inner self throughout your day.

Take the piece of paper and draw a symbol on it that has meaning for you—perhaps a pentacle, a particular rune, a tree leaf, or any other image that resonates for you with magical energy. If you like, use markers or crayons to color in or around the symbol—feel free to infuse it with as much artistic power as you can!

Place the symbol next to the candle, being careful not to burn the paper.

Next, take a small pinch of the dried herbs or flowers and rub it between your palms for a few seconds. Then clap your hands together, allowing the crumbled herbs to fall away and sprinkle around your work area. (It's fun to let a few specks land in the candle flame, but not necessary).

Place the remaining herbs in the charm bag. Take each crystal, one at a time, and hold it in your dominant hand.

Feel yourself sending your purest, strongest magical power into each stone, and then place it in the charm bag.

Finally, add the symbol to the bag, and pull the strings to close it.

Hold it in your hands, gaze into the candle flame, and say these words (or similar words of your own):

> *"As within, so without*
> *Let my connection to spirit never be in doubt*
> *As above, so below*
> *I bring this magic wherever I go"*

Place the charm bag next to the candle and leave it there until the candle burns all the way out on its own. It is now fully charged and ready to go!

NEXT STEPS

As you begin to incorporate the Craft more and more into your lifestyle, you may start considering making a formal commitment of some kind. In the next section, we'll examine the process of initiation into the Craft. We'll start with a look at some basic aspects of the coven experience, and then offer possible avenues for solitary practitioners.

Remember that there's no rush to enact a formal ritual to mark your relationship with this highly personal spiritual practiced. But if it feels right to you, it can be a wonderful milestone on your ongoing journey.

PART TWO

INITIATION AND SELF-DEDICATION

WHAT IS INITIATION?

For most people, the word "initiation" brings to mind a ritual or ceremony in which a person is admitted into a specific organization, usually of a secretive nature.

If your aim is to join a traditional coven, then this is an apt description. However, if you're a solitary Witch, the terminology for this important step along your path is a little less clear-cut.

This is because the conventional sense of *initiation*, particularly in the early days of the rise of modern Witchcraft, has involved the passing down of specific traditions from one Witch to another.

In this lineage system, would-be members of a coven will study under the mentorship of initiated, experienced members until they are knowledgeable and practiced enough to participate in coven rituals, and—most importantly—to commit themselves to spiritual fellowship with the group. Once these initiates have advanced enough along the path of their coven's tradition, they may eventually come to initiate new members.

Therefore, most members of traditional covens, especially those within the Wiccan community, hold the view that one cannot be initiated by anyone other than an already-initiated Witch.

Those who practice a solitary form of the Craft may study diligently from books and other resources, and may choose to enact a solitary ritual that acknowledges their decision to pursue this spiritual path, but because they are undertaking their learning and practice on their own, rather than through mentorship from an initiated Witch, they are not seen as being *initiated*.

Instead, the more widely-recognized term for a solitary Witch's formal entrance into the Craft is *self-dedication*. A ritual of self-dedication may resemble aspects of a coven initiation to varying degrees, but because solitary Witches can design and perform this ritual in any way they like, it is a fundamentally different experience.

Self-dedication happens strictly on your own terms. The commitment you're declaring in such a ritual is really to your inner self, to any deities you may incorporate into your practice, and to the divinity of the Universe as you understand it. It's not a commitment to any other person. It's not an entrance into a group of fellow practitioners. Therefore, according to traditionalists, it can't be an initiation.

Of course, there are counter-arguments to be made here. For one thing, the initiatory lineage of any given coven can't be traced back any further than the middle of the 20th century, when modern Wicca was developed. (There may be a small number of non-Wiccan covens that go back further, but if so, they are highly secretive and very unlikely to be openly recruiting new members.) This means that somewhere along the line, a Witch would have had to self-initiate.

And the same thing happens today in communities where new covens are formed without the assistance of an already-initiated leader—clearly, someone has to self-initiate in order to initiate the others.

So while everyone is entitled to their own perspective on the Craft, don't let those who follow a different set of rules determine how you describe your own personal ritual.

If you like the word "initiation," use it. In fact, you might even choose to view the word in light of its second definition: *the action of beginning something*, since when you self-initiate, you are truly setting your journey along the path into motion.

On the other hand, if "self-dedication" makes more sense to you, then go with it. After all, if you're a solitary Witch— especially if you're following an eclectic path—you can call your ritual anything you like.

For the purposes of the discussion below, the terms "self-initiation" and "self-dedication" are considered to be interchangeable.

But first, we'll take a closer look at the coven approach, for those who would like to know more about initiation in its "classic" form.

INITIATION IN TRADITIONAL COVENS

Traditionally, the act of initiation into a coven involves a highly ritualized ceremony.

In keeping with the traditions of secrecy regarding the Craft, the vast majority of covens do not share the details of their rituals with outsiders. That being said, there are some general characteristics that many coven processes have in common—and initiation is indeed a *process*, a series of steps leading to an experience of spiritual transformation that involves, but is not limited to, the moment of the rite itself.

First, there's a period of time in which the would-be initiate meets and spends time with the coven members, learning basic information about the coven's history and the tradition(s) they follow, and generally getting a sense for whether or not this particular group is a good fit.

This is a crucial undertaking, for both the individual and the coven. Unlike a circle, which is a more informal group of Witches who can rotate in and out as it suits their needs, a coven needs its members to be wholly committed to participating in rituals and contributing their energy on a consistent basis.

If you're initiating into a coven, you're asserting that you intend to stay—not necessarily for the rest of your natural life, but potentially so. You will also be forging intense bonds of friendship and spiritual fellowship that cannot be taken lightly. So you and your fellow potential coveners need to be sure not only that you'll get along well, but that you resonate harmoniously with each other on the deepest levels.

If at any point during this time period, you feel that something is "off" in any way, listen to your intuition! Don't be afraid to address any concerns or questions you may have about initiation or any other aspects of coven life. If you don't feel comfortable enough to discuss them, or if doing so doesn't resolve your concerns, then respectfully walk away. It may just not be meant to be, at least at this time.

If you do find a good fit and decide to begin the initiation process, you will then enter a period of study and mentorship with one or more experienced members of the coven.

The length of this process can vary widely, but most Wiccan covens observe the "year and a day" tradition at a minimum. During this time, you'll be immersing yourself in the beliefs and practices followed by the coven, and, depending on the coven's degree of eclecticism, possibly engaging in your own explorations of the mysteries of the Craft as well.

As a result, you will gradually (and sometimes, seemingly suddenly) find yourself changing from the inside out. Your perceptions of the world will be shifting as you awaken to the unseen energies of the Universe. Your relationship with the deities of your chosen path will unfold and strengthen.

You may also experience uncomfortable shifts in your relationships with others in your life, as you become less interested in the distractions of the modern world and focus your energy on your spiritual development.

Don't be concerned about this—those in your life who are meant to stay in your life will eventually adjust. In the meantime, understand this period of discomfort or disharmony as a natural part of the process. While it's true that initiation is all about new beginnings, it also involves an ending of your old way of life. A certain amount of separation from your former mode of existence—whether it's giving up a toxic TV habit or letting go of an unhealthy friendship—is to be expected.

When you encounter self-doubt—and you most likely will—simply calm your mind, allow yourself to sit with the doubt until you can see it clearly, and let it go. You will eventually come back to your center and remember that you're honoring your truest self by following this path.

As the date of your initiation draws near, you will likely be instructed on how to make your specific preparations for the rite. Again, this will vary widely, but the process usually involves some kind of cleansing or purification ritual, which may be in the form of a bath or shower, or a more symbolic cleansing. Meditation in the days and/or hours before the ceremony is another key component, as you will want to have a clear, calm, and focused mind going into the experience.

Depending on the coven's traditions, the ritual itself may involve the full coven or just a few members, and may be very elaborate or quite simple. Regardless of the specific form it takes, the focus of the ritual will be on acknowledging your commitment to the path of the Craft the coven follows, the deities the coven worships, and spiritual fellowship with the coven members themselves. This declaration is then honored by the coven by welcoming you into the fold, usually accompanied by a celebration of some kind.

While you may not know much about the details prior to the actual event, you should have a general sense of what will transpire.

For example, in some Wiccan covens, initiates are naked (also known as "skyclad") and blindfolded, with arms lightly bound behind them. (The coven members may or may not be skyclad.) This is to solidify the bonds of love and trust between the initiate and the coven, as well as the initiate and the deities. This tradition goes back to the beginnings of Gardnerian Wicca and is not practiced universally, but it's common enough to warrant mentioning here.

If the coven you're joining practices skyclad, you should be aware of this ahead of time, and you should be very comfortable and sure of the people you are working with. Ritual nudity has, unfortunately, attracted sexual predators to the Craft. Abuse of the practice isn't a common occurrence, and if you've been listening to your intuition throughout your journey with the coven, then it's highly unlikely that any unsavory energy would go undetected for this long.

Nonetheless, it's important to look out for yourself. If at any point in the proceedings you feel threatened or unsafe, or if anyone tells you to do anything you're uncomfortable doing, then don't be afraid to walk away right then and there. You can still honor what you've learned from this experience, and trust the Universe to connect you with the right group of people when it's the right time to do so.

Once you're initiated, you will be responsible for keeping your commitments to the coven—to show up for rituals and other meetings, to honor any vows of secrecy, and to be part of the support system that coven membership offers. Depending on the coven you belong to, there may be also further opportunities for structured advancement in your studies, in the form of a degree system.

This is usually found in traditional Wiccan covens, though some non-Wiccan forms of the Craft also observe some kind of tiered system, whether they use the word "degree" or different terminology. Witches who choose to pursue their studies formally in this way will usually go through additional initiation rituals to mark their achievements, and in many cases this is required for any Witch who wishes to initiate others.

Of course, in the widely diverse world of the Craft, there also are plenty of covens that operate without any kind of hierarchy, so if you have a strong preference one way or the other, this is definitely something to consider before beginning your initiation process.

It should be clear by now that initiation into a coven is not something to be taken lightly. You are entering into very strong emotional and spiritual bonds with the individuals in this group, so you need to be extremely compatible with them.

In fact, some Witches have likened initiation to marriage, and many people find that they are closer their fellow coveners than they are to their own family. So don't ever join a coven just because you want to belong to a group of Witches, or you are likely to regret your choice.

Indeed, it's definitely better to practice on your own than to become bound to a situation that is anything less than joyful, caring, and fulfilling.

If your desire is truly to belong to a coven, but the right opportunity hasn't yet come your way, take that as a signal from the Universe that it just isn't time yet. In the meantime, you can find other ways to connect with like-minded souls, such as through an informal Witches' circle or even an online community. You can also still devote yourself to studying the Craft on your own, and self-initiate/self-dedicate whenever it feels right to you.

If and when you do end up finding (or even forming) your ideal coven, you can then undergo a new initiation, if you choose. But whatever the case, know that you do not need another person to initiate you in order for you to "become" a Witch, no matter what anyone says.

INITIATION IN SOLITARY PRACTICE

Although solitary initiation, or self-dedication, is a very different experience from that of a coven initiation, there are still important parallels on the journey to this milestone on your path.

First, of course, is the work of really getting a feel for the Craft—exploring possible avenues in terms of established traditions, getting a sense for what resonates with you and what doesn't, etc.

But while you may choose to communicate and even spend time with people who share your interests during this time (and you may even already have friends who do), ultimately you're still sorting out for yourself what you want your relationship with the Craft to feel like, without also having to determine whether you want to join forces with others in an official way.

You will also, no doubt, experience internal shifts that end up causing some (or even all) of your interpersonal relationships to change, as well as any elements of your lifestyle that may be interfering with your connection to your inner self and your pursuit of the Craft.

There is also some overlap in terms of preparing for the ritual, namely meditation and cleansing or purification—or at least, it's highly recommended that you incorporate these elements.

But such recommendations are just that—there is no real prescribed path, no set of absolute instructions, no one to show you exactly what to do, and no one to do it but you.

This is the chief difference in a solitary initiation, and for many Witches, it's the chief appeal of solitary practice in general. However, others find the lack of established protocol daunting, wishing instead to be led by more experienced practitioners.

Luckily, there are plenty of ways to approach self-dedication with a reasonable amount of structure, if that's your preference. You can find books and online resources that will offer you a well-defined path, from actual interactive classes to recommended book lists, and more.

If you're looking to follow a specific, established practice rather than building your own eclectic form, you can find some good contemporary models, such as Raymond Buckland's *Complete Book of Witchcraft*, or Scott Cunningham's *Wicca: A Guide for the Solitary Practitioner.*

Both of these classic books cover a wide range of elements of the Craft and plenty of practical information, including detailed rituals for self-dedication that you can follow to the letter, if you wish.

And while it's true that you cannot really access the kind of information found only in lineage-based, oath-bound coven traditions, such as Gardnerian Wicca, the practices outlined in these resources are rooted in various branches of these earlier forms, including Gardnerian and Alexandrian Wicca.

If you're seeking a decidedly non-Wiccan path, there are also established traditions such as Italian-based Stregheria, Cochrane's Craft, and contemporary Sabbatic Craft. You can also explore the Feri tradition, an older form that does require study with an initiate to truly learn the heart of it, but does not require coven participation.

If you're more eclectically inclined, you will most likely want to borrow from more than one tradition as you develop your practice, rather than adopting a single form or following a specific course. But you can still set yourself a course of study to follow as you work your way toward the point where you feel ready for initiation. Many solitaries find the year-and-a-day tradition very useful as a means of establishing some structure to their endeavor.

You can also "assign" yourself a certain amount of reading per week, organize your studies around specific topics such as the Wheel of the Year, and/or read all the books written by a particular author before moving on to a new one. Then again, you may want to be more free-wheeling and unmethodical about your study, following your inner guide from moment to moment until you're thoroughly inspired to perform your self-dedication.

When it comes to the ritual itself, if you haven't found one you want to follow in any of the sources you've consulted, then you will need to design your own. You may want to piece one together from various sources, possibly including some details from your own inspiration. Or, you might invent one entirely from scratch.

Below is an example "template" ritual that follows a fairly standard form, yet allows for you to tailor it to suit your individual path.

A RITUAL FOR SELF-INITIATION/ SELF-DEDICATION

This ritual is designed for the solitary practitioner of a non-specific form of Witchcraft. You can follow the instructions below to the letter, or you can use it as a template for creating your own self-dedication ritual.

Because not all Witches recognize a Goddess and/or God, the language used to address and describe "the powers that be" is intentionally open-ended.

Those wishing to acknowledge or emphasize their deities can tailor the wording to suit this purpose. For example, you may be dedicating yourself to "the gods" rather than "the path."

This is a highly personal undertaking, so spend some time thinking about how you want to verbalize your commitment.

THE PREPARATION

Here are a few things for you to consider prior to the self-initiation.

Choose a Date

You might find yourself inspired to enact your self-dedication immediately, but it's best to plan ahead and honor the process of preparing for it, especially if you want it to have a lasting impact.

Choose a date that has some significance for you, either personally or in terms of what's happening in the cosmos. A new moon is an ideal time, but you might also wish to coordinate it with a solstice, or with the beginning of a new astrological sign.

Whatever you decide, give yourself at least a week ahead of time to prepare.

Choose a Place

If you can find an outdoor location in a natural setting where you can be sure you won't be disturbed, this is ideal—even if it's just your backyard. But don't think for a minute that you can't have an equally powerful experience indoors—what matters is that you are alone and in quiet surroundings.

Perhaps you already have a sacred space and/or an altar established in your home—if so, this is a perfect place. If not, consider creating a sacred space for yourself as a first step in your preparations.

You will then be able to return to this space again and again for rituals and spellwork.

Prepare Your Inner Self

For at least one week leading up to the date of your ritual, spend at least a few minutes every day in meditation, preferably at the same time each day.

After you come out of meditation, take a few moments to contemplate your spiritual aspirations. Why are you choosing to formally dedicate yourself to the Craft? What is it, exactly, that you want to communicate to the Universe and/or your deities through the enactment of this ritual? And how do you imagine you will feel afterward?

Take some time to visualize and then practice *feeling* your connection to the magical energies of the Divine.

Do some free writing about your experiences thus far—learning about the Craft, discovering your path, exploring magic, etc.—and about what you would like to see unfold in the future.

As you write, you may come up with some words and phrases that you can use in your ritual, in addition to or instead of the words offered below.

Gather Your Tools

If your ritual takes place inside, you'll need the following:

- 6 tea lights (in holders)

- 1 white pillar candle

- Small bowl of salt or soil

- Anointing oil. This can be a purchased blend, or a homemade blend of essential oil and carrier oil, such as almond or olive oil. (Do not use essential oils directly on skin—mix them with a carrier oil first.) Sandalwood, frankincense, and myrrh are often used for initiation rites, but use a scent that is pleasing to you. And if you don't have access to essential oils, you can simply use olive oil on its own.

- Paper and pen/pencil for writing down your ritual words. (This is optional, but it's recommended to either have this memorized, or have it with you on paper so you don't scatter mental energy trying to remember what to say.)

If you're outside, you don't need the salt or soil, and depending on location and weather conditions, you may want to scale down on the candles. Just one is fine, but if even this isn't possible, you can use an upturned flashlight, or make the shape of a flame with your palms pressed together, fingers pointing to the sky.

A note on clothing: many Witches perform their self-dedication skyclad. If this is possible and you're comfortable with it, go for it. If you have ritual robes, that can be a powerful alternative.

Really, you should wear whatever feels right to you, but do make sure you choose something to wear that marks this occasion somehow. In other words, don't self-dedicate wearing what you wore to work or school that day.

And if at all possible, go barefoot—especially if you're inside.

THE RITUAL

Just before you're ready to begin, take a ritual cleansing bath (or shower) with sea salt. (You can salt a washcloth for use in the shower.)

Visualize the mundane details of your day dissolving, and imagine that you're clearing away any unwanted aspects of your old life, before you discovered your new path.

Afterward, sit in meditation for 5 to 10 minutes to clear your mind. Take some long, slow deep breaths to ground and center yourself.

When you're ready, arrange the tea lights in a circle around you and place the pillar candle in front of you. Sprinkle the salt or soil onto the floor within the circle. Light the tea lights, then stand with your feet in the salt or earth. Take another few deep breaths.

Now it's time to announce your intention formally to the Universe. You can say the following words, or words of your own:

"I stand upon the Earth in this time, in this place,
to declare my dedication to my path of the Craft.
I now release any doubt, old fears, old limiting beliefs,
and any and all resistance to fully embracing this new life."

Now, anoint yourself with the oil, starting with the pulse points of your wrists and neck, then the center of your brow, and finally your heart. (Some traditions go further and anoint eyelids, lips, hands, genitals, and the soles of the feet—do what seems right for you.)

Be very present for this, really focusing on the feel of the oil on your skin—this is the action that symbolizes the joining of your physical self with the non-physical energy of the Universe.

When you're finished, say the following words, or words of your own:

> *"I welcome my sacred connection to the Earth,*
> *and give thanks for the life-sustaining gifts of her abundance.*
> *I dedicate myself to the wisdom of the Craft,*
> *and to continued growth and learning.*
> *I welcome constant communion with the divine.*
> *I embrace the change I am making in this time and place.*
> *I welcome this initiation into the mysteries of the Divine All.*
> *I rejoice in my path."*

To seal your dedication, light the pillar candle. Close with these (or your own) words:

> *"From now on, I walk my path with purpose,*
> *joyfully aware of my divine connection to All That Is."*

Sit still for several moments and bask in the glow of the energetic connection you have just created.

If you're outdoors, listen for bird calls, wind stirring the trees, or any other signals that the natural world is responding to your energy. If you're indoors, gaze softly at the candle flame and watch how it dances in celebration of your actions.

After your ritual, avoid going straight into any mundane activity for the rest of the day (such as cleaning, watching TV or checking social media). Do something special to celebrate, instead.

And from now on, be intentionally open to a new level of connection with the spirit world. You have sent forth a very powerful intention, and that divine love will be returned to you in new and surprising ways.

MOVING FORWARD

As you can see, initiation can take many forms, and is truly a process rather than just a single event. It can be seen as a beginning, but it can also be seen as an honoring of the progress you've made along your path thus far, even as you are stepping into new territory.

If you've prepared yourself adequately and taken the ritual seriously, by being truly present to it and trusting your own process, then you will very likely feel that a change has taken place. Joyous, excited, invigorated, renewed—these are just a few of the words Witches have used to describe their state of mind in the days following their initiation/dedication. But what happens now?

If you've initiated into a coven, you'll most likely be receiving and assimilating new knowledge, and participating in group ritual and magic on a new level. But if you're solitary, your life may not seem a whole lot different—at least, not in any obvious ways.

Don't be alarmed if this is the case. The truth is that, coven or no coven, an initiation ritual is not going to suddenly transform you into a full-time Witch all by itself.

It's still, and always will be, a process. You will still be responsible for your own continued learning and growth, and your own level of participation in active communion with the deities and/or the force(s) of energy you work with. As a solitary, it will still be up to you to celebrate the full moon, to work a spell, to meditate, and to explore new ways of approaching ritual and magic.

If you can remember back to Part One, we discussed the challenges faced by the aspiring Witch—one of the biggest being the difficulty of finding the time to immerse yourself in a "*witchy*" lifestyle. Many of us *want* to practice Witchcraft daily, but life gets in the way.

The act of initiation can bring in powerful inspiration for continuing your practice of the Craft. But acting on that inspiration will still be your decision, with each step of your long and winding path.

Part Three was created for anyone looking to deepen their involvement with the Craft, by making it part of your daily routines. In it, we'll explore some ideas and practices that, over time, can deeply enrich your day to day life as a Witch, expand your capacity to attract magical manifestations, and navigate your way through challenging times.

You might view these offerings as inspiration for your next steps in the post-initiation life. However, this next section is intended to be just as useful for those who have not yet reached this milestone, and even for those who do not choose to make initiation a goal. You can think of it as a collection of "tips for the trail," no matter where you are on yours!

PART THREE
GUIDEPOSTS

A WAY OF LIFE

This guide began with the metaphor of "the path" to describe the process of discovering, learning about, and developing a practice of Witchcraft.

Within this metaphor, the act of initiation is seen as a highly significant point, or milestone, that celebrates your decision to commit to moving forward on your path, whether it be through an established Craft tradition or your own individualized form.

But no matter how your process unfolds, this path is ideally experienced as a way of life, rather than merely as a series of rituals marking the phases of the moon and the journey of the sun around the Earth.

You can go through the motions and follow all the spells and rites you find in your favorite books, but this won't necessarily cause your spiritual self—your delightful *witchiness*—to come through for you in an authentic, deeply felt way.

Ultimately, what we might call "spiritual satisfaction" occurs through being awake and aware on your path as much as possible. Just as you wouldn't spend a nature hike staring only at the ground just ahead of your feet, you don't want to miss the sights and sounds, the beautiful vistas and the quiet, sacred moments of a life in the Craft.

And the more you are available to perceive and allow these moments, the more they will occur, until eventually you are feeling the magical undercurrents of the world around you far more often than not.

This state of being can be achieved by developing new habits of perception that put you more in touch with your sixth sense more of the time, developing and strengthening your inner knowing and opening you up to experiencing more evidence of the inherent magic of the Universe.

There are countless avenues toward this pursuit, which include meditation, divination, journaling, petitioning your deities, spirit guides, or any other energies you work with for guidance, and observing and appreciating the positive manifestations—both material and immaterial—of your practice.

It's also rewarding to develop and maintain your receptivity to messages from the unseen world, which will help you navigate your way along your path. The Universe is constantly providing signs and signals to you in your everyday experience, from subtle affirmations that you're on the right track, to gentle (or not so gentle) warnings to reconsider your current course of action. Depending on your level of receptivity, you may or may not recognize these moments for what they are—but with practice, you definitely will.

Depending on your beliefs, you may experience these messages as being from specific spirit guides, ancestors, elemental energies, or deities—and there can be different messages from different sources— or you might just perceive them to be from "the Universe."

We'll use this last term below for the sake of simplicity, as we explore a few ways in which you can discover the magic of seemingly ordinary moments. These practices do not belong strictly to the realm of Witchcraft, but they share plenty of territory, and they inform the practice of many a Witch.

Like the study and practice of Tarot, runes, and other traditional forms of divination, these are methods of inviting communication from the spirit world. But unlike those active modes, which you can initiate with a question whenever you want to, these are more passive—or receptive—in that your only role is simply to observe and be open.

ANIMAL MESSENGERS

In the ancient world, animals were widely understood to have spirits, or souls, of their own. In myths and stories from around the globe, animals have interacted with human beings, and have even been responsible for the actual creation of the Universe.

In these traditions, animals were not subordinate to humans, but equals. Humans derived benefit from their association with animals, not only in the form of food, clothing, and other goods made from their bodies, but in the form of spiritual protection and wisdom as well.

Many cultures had specific "clan animals" or "totems" to represent distinct groups within their societies, as well as individual animal allies or helpers, variously known as spirit animals, power animals, or totem animals. These relationships between animals and humans are found in Norse, Celtic, and Native American traditions, among many others, and are still honored in living shamanic cultures today.

To some extent, the concept of spirit animals has spread to modern Witchcraft. Of course, the lore of the Craft in Western Europe is full of tales of animal "familiars," but much of it is either Christianized, fancifully exaggerated, or both, so it's hard to know what relationships between Witches and familiars truly entailed.

Still, many Witches today work with animals in both physical and spiritual form. Many deities from the ancient pantheons have long been associated with specific animals, and Witches who work with these deities may choose to use images of the deity's animal in ritual or spellwork.

In some forms of magic, the essence, or spirit of an animal, such as the wolf, the bear, or the eagle can be called upon to aid or guide the work. And plenty of Witches share their homes with cats, birds, and other companion animals who are part of their magical lives.

In recent decades, many Witches have adopted the shamanic belief that everyone has specific spirit animals. It's said that a few of these stay with us from birth to death, but others will come and go from our lives as our circumstances change. Whether or not you incorporate this belief into your practice, it's definitely worth paying attention to animal symbolism as a means of spiritual messaging.

If you study their behavior, you'll find that animals have useful lessons to offer people regarding how to live successfully on Earth. So if a particular animal keeps popping up into your awareness, it's likely that that animal has some advice to offer you.

For example, squirrels are thought to bring a message of the importance of balancing work and play. Alternatively, they may be signaling that you need to be sure your material bases are covered. The spider is a reminder of the virtues of patience and persistence, as well as the importance of viewing a situation from every angle.

Animals can also serve as omens, offering information about a present or future situation. The crow, long associated with warnings of death, can also appear to those on the spiritual path on the eve of some kind of personal transformation. The deer can point to an upcoming new adventure and let you know that you are being gently encouraged to take advantage of it.

Furthermore, your deceased loved ones in the spirit world can, and often do, come to you in the form of animals. This happens most often with birds, butterflies, and other brightly-colored animals that stay in your presence for just a short time. So if you've ever "felt" the presence of someone on the other side when a particular animal is around, you can bet that you received a visit!

If you're not already tapped into the magical realm of animal communication, start being more aware of how animals figure into your experience. This includes animals who literally cross your path in your daily life, as well as those you encounter in dreams and in other imagery.

There is a wealth of information in books and online sources you can turn to for interpretations of these animal communications, so you can always look up any animal that catches your attention. Of course, not every sighting of an animal is necessarily significant—as they say, sometimes a bird is just a bird. But if a particular animal starts showing up in your life repeatedly, consider the possibility that it's trying to tell you something.

Sometimes it will be quite obvious that there's a message, such as when a wild animal "randomly" enters your house, or when you're having recurring dreams about the same animal. But often it can be subtle.

Perhaps you keep seeing giraffes in various unrelated posts on social media, and then a birthday card arrives in the mail with a giraffe on the cover. Or maybe you keep seeing robins whenever you're worrying about a particular problem in your life.

These moments can be seen as invitations to pause, take a step back, and seek a new perspective on whatever has been going on in your life. They could also be signals to stay open to new developments that are just around the corner.

Take a moment to communicate with the spirit energy of any animal that crosses your path in a distinctive way. Thank it for visiting you, and do some research to find out more specifically what it has to say to you. As you make a deliberate practice of these observations, you will find that the Universe responds by sending you even more messages from the animal kingdom.

"SCRYING" IN NATURE

The term "scrying" usually refers to the art of seeing images in a reflective surface, for the purposes of divination.

Like much of magic, scrying is a skill that takes practice—very few beginners are able to gaze into a crystal ball and instantly get results. It's also harder than other forms of divination, such as Tarot cards or runes, because there's no system of specific images and associated meanings to work with.

Instead, what the scryer sees in the crystal, mirror, or bowl of water could literally be *anything*, and only the scryer can interpret the images and symbols, which makes it a very personal and individualized process.

But whether or not you have interest or ability in the art of scrying itself, this concept can be used to open up a wealth of opportunities to interact with the magical energy of the natural world. Nature offers countless "surfaces" for seeing images in, and not just glassy lakes, ponds and puddles. You can receive stunning visual messages from gazing with a soft focus at flames, clouds, trees, and just about anything else you see.

Looking at nature in this way helps you to exercise a weaker intuitive "muscle," as you rely exclusively on your visual perception, with no need for language—and this is particularly good for people with highly analytical and/or verbal minds.

What you see when you practice this subtle art may be reflecting something about your inner process or present circumstances, but it may also just be about connecting with the divine mystery, allowing your spirit to engage in some much-needed "play time."

No matter where or how you grew up, you almost certainly spent time as a child watching the clouds for shapes and faces as they floated by. This is perhaps the easiest and most common form of "nature-scrying," and was practiced by our ancestors probably since the dawn of humanity.

While clouds of any type or size can create a good canvas in any kind of weather, there's something particularly magical about large, thick clouds with a lot of color variation due to storms or sunlight, as these can produce the most complex and stunning images.

Fast-moving clouds are also wonderful for their ability to keep changing "the scene" as they sail by! In fact, in the right circumstances, the sky can seem to be putting on a lively and action-packed drama with multiple characters and stories.

If you abandoned the practice of cloud-watching after you left childhood, now is a good time to pick it back up. The next time you find yourself with 10 or 15 minutes free on a good cloud-watching day, go outside and just stare up at the sky.

Let go of any current worries and distractions and let your focus soften as the clouds pass over you. What shapes and/or images can you see? How are the edges of the clouds interacting with each other? Don't try to force any images to become recognizable to you as anything in particular. Simply watch the show and see what arises.

Clouds may seem to be among the most obvious natural scrying tools, but trees also offer excellent "canvases," particularly in the summer months when they are fully fleshed out with leaves. If you soften your gaze when looking at them, you'll likely find that all kinds of faces pop out— among the leaves as well as on trunks and branches.

Many people fondly refer to these faces as "the faeries," while others see them as representations of the Goddess and God. Plenty of other shapes can also appear, most often those of animals.

As with cloud-watching, windy days can be particularly good for scrying among leafy trees, since the images can change rapidly with the wind's movement. But it isn't strictly necessary for there to be leaves on the trees, nor does it have to be daytime—the stark contrast of bare branches against the moonlit sky can also create fantastic magical imagery.

So next time you're blessed to have one or more trees in your view, start taking notice of what you can see in the leaves, branches, and trunks. If there are trees visible from a window where you live, pay attention to the images that arise at various times of the day and the year.

Stones are another great source of naturally-occurring imagery. Whether you're gazing at large boulders in a natural setting, or examining small rocks you've picked up along hikes, you can find plenty of images in the lines and color variations found in common stones.

Many stones—and seashells for that matter—from certain geological areas contain tiny fossils of organisms millions of years old. These delightful images can be thought of as ancient "postcards" from past eras!

One nice aspect of these more permanent works of art is that you can look at them again and again, unlike the more fleeting images you see in clouds and trees. But temporary canvases can be just as compelling, whether they be in the sky or on the ground—such as the patterns on a shoreline made from incoming waves, or tracks made by animals in the snow.

And let's not forget the classic and perhaps most magical scrying source known to humans—fire! Whether it's a boisterous bonfire or the quiet flame of a single flickering candle, the imagery found within fire can be truly mesmerizing.

Really, once you get into the habit of viewing so much of the world in this way, you can start seeing shapes and faces in just about anything that has variations in lines and/or coloring, whether it's a natural object or not.

For example, some Witches like to examine the melted wax of spent candles for messages about the outcome of their spellwork. You can even see images in melting butter or oil in a skillet with the right perceptual awareness!

The psychological term for this ability is "pareidolia," which is usually defined as a tendency to interpret something known or familiar from a stimulus where it doesn't actually exist. (This is what explains the sometimes widely-publicized phenomena of people seeing the face of Jesus or Mary in a piece of toast.) Some of these images, like the "man on the Moon," can be perceived by whole populations, while others are only recognizable to one person.

But while scientists may only be interested in the brain functions involved in this process, Witches and other intuitives know that there's something larger going on. It could be argued that the Universe is just one giant tapestry of imagery and message, always communicating, and always alive to new interpretations from new recipients of the information it offers.

As you practice seeing in this way, it's possible that you'll perceive images that seem to indicate negativity, such as unsmiling or even seemingly-menacing faces in a cloud or the trunk of a tree.

Don't get swept up in interpreting these visions from a place of fear. There could be many reasons for what you perceive as "negative" messaging.

For example, you may be picking up a reflection of a feeling within yourself, such as the dread of an upcoming exam or sadness after an argument with a friend. You might also simply be misunderstanding the energy of the image due to cultural conditioning.

Most of us have been trained to see a smile as the only real positive facial expression, and may assume that any other type of expression indicates unhappiness or negativity. But if you look at artistic representations of deities, spirits, faeries, or other manifestations of the invisible world—particularly those from pre-modern times—you will often see unsmiling faces on these benevolent beings. So don't automatically assume that a less-than-joyous image is an "ill omen."

In fact, this practice is just as much an exercise in perception as a way of receiving specific information. It's about training your mind to look past the ordinary, expected view of the objects in your world, and opening your awareness to the subtle, less-seen aspects of reality.

As you develop this practice over time, you may find that there is a pattern of correspondence between what you see and what you're experiencing in your life, but even then, not every image you see in a cloud or a stone is going to be a significant communication meant just for you. Sometimes a face is just a face. The point is that you're strengthening your connection to the Universe by being receptive to its subtle beauty.

THE MAGIC OF NUMBERS

Have you ever had times in your life when you seem to "randomly" look at the clock at the same time every day? Or times when the same number keeps popping up in many different ways in a short span of time?

Maybe you see the same pattern of numbers repeatedly, such as sequential sets (123, 987, etc.) or triple digits (444, 222, etc.) Or perhaps you keep coming across numbers that are personally significant to you—such as the digits of your birthday, or the address of your childhood home.

Whatever the case, if specific numbers are showing up in your life in unusual or otherwise noticeable ways, then you can safely assume that the Universe is trying to tell you something.

Numerical messages can be delightful "puzzles" to work out. Even if you've never had much interest in numerology, the meanings of numbers on their own are worth investigating when particular numbers are getting your attention.

You don't need to delve into the various ways in which numerologists assign and interpret your personal numbers, which generally have to do with your date of birth and the letters of your name—although that information can be illuminating as well for those who are interested. Simply having a look into the ways in which the numbers themselves are interpreted can open up a new world of understanding about where you are in your present life circumstances, and/or what the Universe is nudging you to learn about yourself.

For example, the number 8 is said to symbolize abundance and success. The number 5 can point to unpredictability and action, while 6 often deals with matters of relationships. Double and triple digit numbers also carry significance. If you're seeing the number 17 over and over again, this can be a hint that you need to work to stay true to your core spiritual values. Repeated sightings of 111 is a signal that what you're currently focusing on is being manifested, so paying attention to your thoughts is important at this time.

The most common places people see recurring numbers are on digital clocks, license plates, phone numbers, advertisements, and other signage, but they can also show up in other ways. You may come across a number repeatedly as you're reading or flipping through channels on the television, or hear it mentioned aloud by people in conversation.

A number can manifest not just as a numeral, but in other ways as well. For example, on a nature hike, some people might attribute meaning to the number of birds in a small flock flying overhead, or the number of trees in a sacred grove. For others, passing four of the exact same type of vehicle in a row on the highway may have significance.

Of course, Witches have long understood that numbers are powerful. Plenty of spellwork makes use of numbers in various ways. For example, the number of crystals or candles called for is generally quite intentional, as is the number of times a phrase or gesture is repeated.

The number three is particularly significant in many Wiccan forms of the Craft, as is seen in the Threefold Law and the Triple Goddess. Thirteen, of course, is also powerful for many in the Craft, and some Witches also highly value the number seven, as it has quite a lot of significance in religious and spiritual traditions around the world.

As you develop your own practice, consider keeping the energetic power of numbers in your awareness. You can find plenty of information about numerical symbolism online and in print resources, from a variety of spiritual systems—the classical numerology of the Western Mystery Tradition is just one option.

You'll most likely find a few different possible interpretations depending on where you look, but your intuition will help you discern which meaning is relevant to you and your situation. And no matter where you look for help in deciphering the message, once a number gets your attention and you begin exploring its significance, you'll find it popping up with even more frequency.

Keep in mind, of course, that just as with any other aspect of tuning into Universal messages, it's possible to go overboard, so beware of becoming obsessed with numbers! You can definitely become unnecessarily distracted if you're looking for a "sign" in every single number you come across in your daily life.

But if you've never given much thought to numbers before, it's worth starting to acquaint yourself with these timeless symbols, since they provide so many opportunities for the Universe to support you on your path.

READING THE SIGNS

There are infinite ways in which the mysterious energies of the unseen world can show up in your life.

It may happen in the form of psychic connections, such as when you're thinking of a friend or relative who then suddenly calls you out of the blue. Often it occurs as a series of seeming coincidences—or what others might call synchronicity or serendipity.

For example, you may hear a song on the radio with lyrics that perfectly describe your present circumstances in an eerie way. Or perhaps a specific book title or movie is mentioned in several different, unrelated conversations throughout your day.

Although these occurrences happen to everyone, they seem to be more pronounced and interesting for those who find themselves drawn to the Craft. However, being a Witch doesn't automatically make you more adept at understanding what, if anything, the messages are supposed to mean.

So how *do* you know whether something is a "sign," or just an interesting or odd coincidence? When is a bird just a bird?

This can be challenging to discern, since each person has a unique, individual relationship with the Universe and no two people experience these messages in the same way. However, there are a few factors to consider when you find yourself unsure about whether you're on the receiving end of divine communication.

First and foremost, check in with your gut.

Are you truly *feeling* a sense of significance around this event, or is it more like simple amusement? If you have a strong intuitive sense that something more is going on here, than you're probably correct. But if that intuitive "tug" isn't really present, then there's no need to give the occurrence further thought.

Another aspect to consider is the frequency and form of the occurrence. For example, hearing the same song on the radio repeatedly throughout the day is hardly unusual if it's a popular song in heavy rotation. But hearing a much lesser-known song a few times may be another story, particularly if you're hearing it in different and unexpected places.

Another example might be a specific phrase in a book that catches your attention, then later turns up in an unrelated conversation with a friend, and later still in a commercial. In other words, coincidences with a high degree of both frequency and improbability can generally be assumed to be more than just coincidence.

For most of us, the ability to identify and interpret messages from the spirit world comes gradually, with practice. Unless you were born with highly developed psychic gifts, this will often feel like guesswork, at least in the beginning.

But it's well worth the effort to keep at it, as you'll be developing two important and related elements of your experience along your path: a stronger connection to your intuition, and a personalized "vocabulary" through which you can receive information from the Universe, which may include animal visits, visions in the trees, numerological messages, and/or other mysterious events.

You'll truly be able to recognize and affirm those magical moments when the spirit world is giving you, and only you, a warm wink and a nod.

A WITCH'S JOURNAL— KEEPING MAGICAL RECORDS

If you're reading this guide, you have most likely already experienced plenty of interesting, and even exhilarating moments of magic in your life—moments when you've known that you're exactly where you're supposed to be, when you're sure that some unseen force is trying to tell you something, when evidence of a successful spell manifests, or when you've witnessed something that could only be explained as a "miracle."

While nearly everyone has had an experience or two like this at some point in their lives that they never forget, there are actually plenty of magical moments happening all around us that can easily go unnoticed—or briefly registered and then were forgotten.

Letting these occurrences slide under the radar of your awareness, however relatively insignificant they may seem, is like wasting perfectly good evidence of your magical connection to the Universe. Then, during those tough days or weeks that feel decidedly "unmagical" due to difficult circumstances, you may begin to have doubts about your belief in magic and/or the Craft. This is a common challenge for aspiring Witches who haven't yet had enough success in magic to keep the flame of their beliefs alive through the more difficult times.

Keeping a written record of your magical moments is a sure-fire way to keep yourself aligned with your path. When you have written evidence of your prior experience, you can use it to silence those negative thought forms that try to dissuade you from your beliefs.

It can be incredibly easy to forget even our most astounding encounters with the spirit world once a stubborn obstacle is staring us straight in the face, but if we've written them down, we can come back to those moments whenever we need a reminder that we really are being supported every step of the way.

What's more, the act of writing about magical moments automatically gives our memory of them more energy—in essence, creating positive thought forms that can be strengthened again every time we read back over what we've written.

And because like attracts like, the more we reinforce our thoughts and feelings around these positive encounters, the more magical moments we're inviting into our lives.

So what constitutes a "magical moment," exactly? What should you be writing down?

The answer varies from person to person, of course, but a general rule of thumb is anything that strikes you as out of the ordinary—an occurrence, however brief or fleeting, that seems to rise above the level of your mundane existence in order to get your attention.

This can include any of the "messaging systems" discussed above, such as interesting or unusual animal sightings, particularly striking images you may have noticed in a cloud or a clear puddle of water, or particular numbers showing up again and again throughout your day or your week.

Any other synchronicities or incidents that seem too strange to chalk up to "coincidence" should also be noted, as well as any significant dreams that you can recall. (Speaking of dreams, it's recommended that you write about your dreams as soon as you can, since the details can often be lost even minutes after you wake up.)

You may be quite unclear as to what any of these occurrences are supposed to "mean" to you as they're happening. This is fine—in fact, it's all the more reason to record them! You may very likely understand, after a few days or weeks have passed, what a particular message or set of messages is indicating.

In fact, the practice of recording and then revisiting these signs can really help you gain an appreciation for what is often called "divine timing." Sometimes, you are being tipped off to unfolding events in advance of their actual manifestation, because the messaging, however unclear it may seem, helps keep you alert enough to avoid being caught off-guard by the unexpected.

Furthermore, over time this practice can help you get a better sense of when "a bird is just a bird," because your intuition will get more finely tuned as you repeatedly ask yourself whether or not a particular occurrence really qualifies for you as a "magical moment."

In addition to the more mysterious signs and signals, be sure to record happy surprises, gifts, blessings—anything that stimulates or reinforces a positive view of your current circumstances is worth appreciating through writing!

It's also crucial to acknowledge any occurrence that can be seen as a manifestation of specific spellwork, even if it doesn't quite seem to hit the target you were aiming for. For example, if you've recently worked a money spell and then start finding coins on the ground or unexpected small bills in the pocket of a coat you haven't worn in awhile, record it—it's a start!

Keeping track of the results of your magic is an excellent way to learn which spells and methods work best for you. You might also want to write down the results of any divination sessions you participate in, such as Tarot readings, as these potentially handy details can often be difficult to recall later on.

How and where you keep your "magical records" is up to you. You might keep a journal specifically for this purpose—a "diary" of your experiences along your path. Or, if you keep a book of shadows, you could jot down the most significant occurrences there—particularly results of spellwork. Depending on your relationship with technology, you might even keep your records electronically—though many Witches would argue for the old-fashioned pen and paper method, as the physical act of handwriting is thought to reinforce the positive energy of recording the evidence of magic.

But no matter how you go about it, try to make it a consistent practice, and be sure to review what you've written from time to time—

particularly when life seems to be short on magic. You'll be amazed at how reassuring it is to see the evidence to the contrary.

PARTING THOUGHTS

Whether you are actively working toward the milestone of initiation, or have already had this experience, or even if you are just continuing to explore the Craft without plans to formally mark your journey, these practices can enrich your life along your path.

As you get into the habit of increasing your awareness of the subtle energetic currents of the unseen world, you will find magic even in the midst of your "humdrum" everyday existence. Over time, you will experience more and more of a seamless weaving of the spiritual and the mundane, rather than an "ordinary" life punctuated by magical moments.

This progression into deeper spiritual territory is really what initiation is all about—the ongoing process of discovery, allowing your relationship with spirit to evolve beyond your expectations. Embrace and enjoy it!

CONCLUSION

Hopefully, this guide has provided helpful advice for navigating the twists and turns of your journey into the wonderful realms of the Craft. Of course, as you know by now, when it comes to the question of where to go next, you are your ultimately your own guide.

But whether you pursue a traditional path to initiation into one or more forms of Witchcraft, or maintain a solitary practice of self-dedication, know that there will always be more to discover.

Even if you end up being drawn to a different path altogether, honor yourself for having invested this time and energy to exploring the interests of your heart. And never doubt that everywhere you look, there is magic to be found.

On that note, I will say goodbye, as it's now time for you to continue on your path. I hope that this book has helped you to take a few more steps forward, and I wish you all the best on the rest of your journey. Keep reading and never stop learning, and who knows where your journey will take you!

Thank you one more time for reading. Blessed Be.

SUGGESTIONS FOR FURTHER READING

Although this list is divided into Wiccan and non-Wiccan categories, there is often some overlap between the two.

Non-Wiccan sources may incorporate elements of Wicca into their practice, but do not identify their traditions as being Wiccan. Because there is less emphasis on initiation in many non-Wiccan forms of the Craft, books on this topic are a bit harder to come by.

Nonetheless, the sources listed below can help you broaden your horizons as they present many possible paths to initiation, self-dedication, and (most importantly) continued learning as you go forward with your journey. Please be aware that there are many more resources available in print and online in addition to these suggestions.

Happy reading!

Wicca

Raymond Buckland, *Buckland's Complete Book of Witchcraft* (1986)

Raymond Buckland, *Wicca for One: The Path of Solitary Witchcraft* (2004)

Scott Cunningham, *Wicca: A Guide for the Solitary Practitioner* (1989)

Janine DeMartini, *A Seeker's Journey and Initiation into Wicca* (2006)

Amethyst Treleven, *Seeker's Guide to Learning Wicca: Training to First Degree in The Northern Hemisphere* (2008)

Amethyst Treleven, *Seeker's Guide to Learning Wicca: Training to First Degree in The Southern Hemisphere* (2008)

Traditional / Non-Wiccan Witchcraft

Victor and Cora Anderson, *The Heart of the Initiate: Feri Lessons* (2012)

T. Thorn Coyle, *Make Magic of Your Life: Passion, Purpose, and the Power of Desire* (2013)

Christopher Penczak, *The Inner Temple of Witchcraft* (2002)

Christopher Penczak, *The Outer Temple of Witchcraft* (2012)

FREE AUDIOBOOK PROMOTION

Don't forget, you can now enjoy a free audiobook version of any of my books when you start a free 30-day trial with Audible. This includes best-sellers such as *Wicca for Beginners* and *Wicca Book of Spells*.

Members receive free audiobooks every month, as well as exclusive discounts. And, if you don't want to continue with Audible, just remember to cancel your membership. You won't be charged a cent, and you'll get to keep your book!

To download this or any of my 20+ books on Wicca and related topics, simply visit:

www.wiccaliving.com/free-audiobook

Happy listening!

MORE BOOKS BY LISA CHAMBERLAIN

Wicca for Beginners: A Guide to Wiccan Beliefs, Rituals, Magic, and Witchcraft

Wicca Book of Spells: A Book of Shadows for Wiccans, Witches, and Other Practitioners of Magic

Wicca Herbal Magic: A Beginner's Guide to Practicing Wiccan Herbal Magic, with Simple Herb Spells

Wicca Book of Herbal Spells: A Book of Shadows for Wiccans, Witches, and Other Practitioners of Herbal Magic

Wicca Candle Magic: A Beginner's Guide to Practicing Wiccan Candle Magic, with Simple Candle Spells

Wicca Book of Candle Spells: A Book of Shadows for Wiccans, Witches, and Other Practitioners of Candle Magic

Wicca Crystal Magic: A Beginner's Guide to Practicing Wiccan Crystal Magic, with Simple Crystal Spells

Wicca Book of Crystal Spells: A Book of Shadows for Wiccans, Witches, and Other Practitioners of Crystal Magic

Tarot for Beginners: A Guide to Psychic Tarot Reading, Real Tarot Card Meanings, and Simple Tarot Spreads

Runes for Beginners: A Guide to Reading Runes in Divination, Rune Magic, and the Meaning of the Elder Futhark Runes

Wicca Moon Magic: A Wiccan's Guide and Grimoire for Working Magic with Lunar Energies

Wicca Wheel of the Year Magic: A Beginner's Guide to the Sabbats, with History, Symbolism, Celebration Ideas, and Dedicated Sabbat Spells

Wicca Kitchen Witchery: A Beginner's Guide to Magical Cooking, with Simple Spells and Recipes

Wicca Essential Oils Magic: A Beginner's Guide to Working with Magical Oils, with Simple Recipes and Spells

Wicca Elemental Magic: A Guide to the Elements, Witchcraft, and Magical Spells

Wicca Magical Deities: A Guide to the Wiccan God and Goddess, and Choosing a Deity to Work Magic With

Wicca Living a Magical Life: A Guide to Initiation and Navigating Your Journey in the Craft

Magic and the Law of Attraction: A Witch's Guide to the Magic of Intention, Raising Your Frequency, and Building Your Reality

Wicca Altar and Tools: A Beginner's Guide to Wiccan Altars, Tools for Spellwork, and Casting the Circle

Wicca Finding Your Path: A Beginner's Guide to Wiccan Traditions, Solitary Practitioners, Eclectic Witches, Covens, and Circles

Wicca Book of Shadows: A Beginner's Guide to Keeping Your Own Book of Shadows and the History of Grimoires

Modern Witchcraft and Magic for Beginners: A Guide to Traditional and Contemporary Paths, with Magical Techniques for the Beginner Witch

FREE GIFT REMINDER

As a thank-you gift to my readers, you can also download a free eBook version of *Wicca: Little Book of Spells.* These ten spells are ideal for newcomers to the practice of magic, but are also suitable for any level of experience!

You can download it by visiting:

www.wiccaliving.com/bonus

I hope you enjoy it!

DID YOU ENJOY
WICCA STARTER KIT?

Thanks so much for reading this book! I know there are many great books out there about Wicca, so I really appreciate you choosing this one.

If you enjoyed the book, I have a small favor to ask—would you take a couple of minutes to leave a review for this book on Amazon?

Your feedback will help me to make improvements to this book, and to create even better ones in the future. It will also help me develop new ideas for books on other topics that might be of interest to you. Thanks in advance for your help!